A Little HISTORY *of* DUBLIN

Trevor Robertson White was born in Dublin in 1972. Educated at Sandford Park, St Columba's College and Trinity College, he worked as a journalist in London and New York before launching *The Dubliner* magazine in 2001. Ten years later he founded the award-winning Little Museum of Dublin, where the story of the city is told in a collection created by public donation. He is the author of three plays and seven books, including *The Dubliner Diaries*, *Malton's Views of Dublin* and *Alfie: The Life and Times of Alfie Byrne*.

A Little
HISTORY
of DUBLIN

TREVOR WHITE

with illustrations by
PHILIP BARRETT

MERRION
PRESS

First published in 2023 by

Merrion Press

10 George's Street

Newbridge

Co. Kildare

Ireland

www.merrionpress.ie

© Text: Trevor Robertson White;
illustrations: Philip Barrett, 2023

978 1 78537 462 3 (Paper)

978 1 78537 463 0 (Ebook)

A CIP catalogue record for this book is
available from the British Library.

Typeset in Minion Pro 11.5/16.5 pt

Cover design by Dara Flynn, Philip Barrett and Barbara Sangster

Merrion Press is a member of Publishing Ireland.

MIX
Paper | Supporting
responsible forestry
FSC® C021394

For SJW

In this high-speed history, the reader is invited to march through time in the company of some expeditious Dubliners. Our story unfolds at an average speed of 6.4 years per page.

Contents

'Dublin is a city of contradictions and survivals. Its biography is not the history of Ireland. Its character has been developed by successive invasions, by prosperity in the eighteenth century and decay in the nineteenth, and by political independence at the present day. Through these phases can be traced its local pride and its conflicting loyalties, its amusements and its grievances; and as it is a city of talkers, due attention must be given to its gossip.'

Christine Longford

Preface

Ireland cannot let go. A fixation with its own baggage is the context in which the media invent some new scandal from time to time, and why this scandal is aired on *Liveline*, a popular but unusual programme in which the scabs of middle Ireland are picked on live radio. The host of the show, Joe Duffy, is himself a part-time historian, which makes sense in a country with no border between history and current affairs. Recently, one of these tiffs – about Ireland's imperial past – prompted Professor Jane Ohlmeyer to write a testy article for *The Irish Times*:

> Ireland was England's first colony. We lived as part of the English, and then British, Empire for over 700 years. The Normans first conquered Ireland in 1169 and aside from a brief decade of independence during the 1640s Ireland formed an integral part of the English imperial system, until 1922 and the foundation of the modern state. As well as being colonised the Irish operated as active colonists in the empires of Britain and other European powers.

In employing such language, Ohlmeyer had a clear sense of her audience: liberal, self-critical, metropolitan. *Irish Times* readers were unlikely to take offence at the 'active colonists' part of her shtick. As the article would not be seen by the plain people of Ireland, the historian would not be attacked on *Liveline* for the crime of blunt speech.

The Irish people are obsessed with the past while seldom considering the vast sweep of all that history because they are not taught English history. It is particularly hard to understand the story of the Irish capital without first considering the experience of the people who live in what is now called England. To understand Dublin, you must first look east.

When the Normans conquered the south of England in 1066, they faced periodic rebellion in the north of England and the Celtic nations, areas that are sometimes called Outer Britain. The south had the better land, the better climate and a quick boat to Europe. It was richer and more prosperous than Outer Britain, and the most recent outbursts of English nationalism can be traced to this ancient gripe.

The history of Ireland, and in particular the history of Dublin, must be seen in that broader context to understand why the 'English', with their own experience of being colonised by the 'French', would try to annex 'Ireland' in the twelfth century. (The inverted commas indicate the looseness of these terms – they are not historically accurate – but the point remains.)

As the inhabitants of England's first colony, the Irish become role-players in a larger set of experiences, with each party struggling to forge its own destiny. It is the fate of all neighbours. England goes on to create an empire by practising a form of moral barbarism that is so polite they almost get away with it. And Dublin was the despised centre of the colonial project in Ireland.

When the Irish rugby team takes to the pitch in Twickenham, all that history crashes into the present. Equally, when a Corkman arrives in Dublin, the past is never far from top of mind. No wonder the quintessential Dublin author James Joyce – the son of a Corkman – called Irish history 'a nightmare from which I am trying to awake'.

Turning away from the convoluted reality of the past is one response to all this head-spinning history. Leaving town is another. It was Joyce who observed that the shortest way to Tara was via Holyhead. But one cannot make sense of Dublin without at least trying to engage with the past. One of the reasons why his masterpiece, *Ulysses*, is so compelling is because Joyce is intimate with the complications of all that history. His position as an Irish nationalist artist who made his home in Europe encouraged him to see the bigger picture: that eclecticism is a signal virtue of *the* great Dublin novel. In this epic account of a day in the life of Leopold Bloom, a half-Jewish Dubliner, the reader recognises why the story of the city demands to be seen in the broadest possible context. The first great multi-hyphenated Dubliner was not Bloom but Joyce himself.

A century after the publication of *Ulysses*, the Irish village that became a Viking town and an English city is the capital of a mature, independent European republic. This short book tells the story of the Hibernian metropolis from its foundation as a village on the banks of the Liffey to its position as the prosperous, multi-ethnic capital of a take-me-for-granted democracy.

Books are the family business. Dublin is particularly well served by its biographers, and the author has consulted many great doorstop histories. *This* is not that sort of book. Designed to be read in an afternoon, this long-short history invites the reader to bring the fullness of time and space to mind – in a single gulp – to measure the scale of a place and its people, occasionally at the same reckless speed as the mannerless seagulls that have colonised St Stephen's Green.

All cities are the remnants of people who had to make room for other people. This book sees Dublin through the eyes of Irish, Viking, Anglo-Norman, Huguenot, Quaker and Jewish *Dubliners*. New blood can change the way we see ourselves, but outsiders can also come from within: from James Joyce to Mary Robinson, this account salutes individuals who have tried to make something more beautiful and more just than an ordinary city.

All manuscripts represent a working out.[1] In this case, the text unpicks the very different stories of Ireland and Dublin. How could a capital be so alien to the state it represents? One answer is that Dublin is an only child, with its own character. *Sui generis.* The playwright Christine Longford wrote that 'its history is not that of Ireland'. But it is also true, as we shall see, that Dubliners are related to everyone. Understanding them will require some flexibility.

The author claims no special licence. As books are central to the story of Dublin, writing a book about Dublin is perhaps

---

1   In these footnotes the diligent reader can expect more history and a few bits of gossip, because Dublin 'is a city of talkers', as Christine Longford wrote in her biography of the city.

the most Dublin thing to do in the world (apart, that is, from talking about writing a book about Dublin). However, this text certainly reflects the author's experience of working in a museum that tells the story of Dublin in twenty-nine minutes, nine times a day, seven days a week. Speed is not just a virtue in the Little Museum. It is a condition of doing business.

So let's get going.

Coming up, 1,500 years in less than 1,500 words: an incomplete history of Dublin in the time it takes to walk the length of O'Connell Street.

The reader is invited to take a deep breath.

A *Very* Little History of Dublin

The first people who came to Ireland probably crossed from Scandinavia to Britain, and then to the north of Ireland via Scotland. It could have been a wrong turn. We know little about these people or their descendants: just enough to marvel at their sophistication.

There were Celts in Dublin before the Vikings arrived, and the Vikings who settled in AD 841 were not the first visitors from that part of the world, but they *were* the first to establish a community. By the twelfth century, Dublin was the largest Viking settlement outside Scandinavia.

In 1166, the King of Leinster, Diarmait Mac Murchada, asked the King of England, Henry II, for help to settle a local feud in Ireland. Mac Murchada successfully engaged an Anglo-Norman mercenary called Strongbow to further his cause, with the blessing of Henry. Sensing a threat to his own authority, though, Henry II came to Dublin and asserted his rule over Strongbow *and* the island of Ireland. This chance-an-arm King gave Dublin to the men of Bristol, inviting them to develop his new possession.

The construction of Dublin Castle gave the Anglo-Norman colonial project a forbidding face. Outside, the poor operated in the twilight zone between begging and scraping by: deprivation is a recurring theme in this story. Famine and plague had disastrous effects – the Black Death wiped out a quarter of Dublin's population – but the city bounced back. This is also a story about unlikely survival.

In the sixteenth and seventeenth centuries, large swathes of Ireland were taken by the English state and given to servants of the new order. In a campaign of ethnic cleansing, Oliver Cromwell sanctioned the deaths of up to one-fifth of the Irish population.

After Cromwell's death, the British monarchy was restored, and James Butler, Duke of Ormond, returned to Dublin to serve as lord lieutenant. The Renaissance arrived in Ireland with Butler, who was the first person to imagine the metropolis that Dublin might become.

In 1690, the Protestant William of Orange beat the forces of the Catholic James II in Meath. A proxy fight for European supremacy, the Battle of the Boyne confirmed the Protestant Ascendancy for centuries to come. It also fuelled a strain of anti-Catholicism that made Anglo-Irish relations more toxic than ever.

The eighteenth century begins with Jonathan Swift – the Dean of St Patrick's Cathedral who put Dublin on the literary map of the world – and continues with a Golden Age, when celebrity architects built Georgian Dublin. This 'gorgeous mask' was a reflection of new prosperity, but there was also staggering poverty.

Some Protestant Huguenots came to Dublin at the end of the century, after fleeing religious persecution in France. Those Huguenots belong on a mantelpiece of new blood alongside other Protestants, as well as Britons and the new Irish from every whisper of the globe. Dubliners are related to everyone.

In the late eighteenth century, some of the most egregious anti-Catholic laws were reformed in the corrupt, unrepresentative parliament on College Green. And by 1800, Dublin was the sixth-largest city in Europe, larger than both Rome and Madrid, with a population of about 200,000.

After an ill-fated rebellion, the 1800 Act of Union saw power removed to London. The Irish parliament was basically bribed into abolishing itself. The political and social elite abandoned Dublin, and the middle classes left for the new suburbs.

There was another rebellion against British rule in 1803. It was led by Robert Emmet, who gave a courtroom speech that a young Oscar Wilde would later recite in town halls all over America. 'When my country takes its place among the nations of the earth, then, and not till then, let my epitaph be written.'

The nineteenth century saw improvements in the governance of the city, the development of the suburbs and the opening of the first commuter railway line. Twelve years after Daniel O'Connell secured Catholic Emancipation in 1829, the City Council elected a Catholic lord mayor in O'Connell himself.

The Great Famine of 1845–52 claimed the lives of a million Irish people and another million were forced to emigrate. Dublin was swamped by internal refugees.

In the 1870s, a Protestant landowner called Charles Stewart Parnell campaigned for Home Rule, a limited form of independence. That same decade, some newcomers arrived in Dublin from Lithuania. This small community of Litvak Jews would establish a lively presence around Portobello.

Dublin was a city of about 270,000 people on 16 June 1904, when James Joyce first walked out with Nora Barnacle. Joyce's portrait of the city on that date, *Ulysses*, is a landmark in the cultural life of Ireland and Europe.

The largest industrial relations dispute in Irish history started in 1913, when men working on the trams put down their badges and began the strike that would become the Dublin Lockout. But the striking men were effectively starved back to work.

Nationalists wanted more. What was the answer to the Irish Question? Home Rule – a limited form of independence – seemed plausible and, eventually, attainable. But the start of the First World War diverted attention: over 200,000 Irishmen served in the British forces during the war. At least 30,000 lost their lives.

In 1916, when rebels launched an insurrection on the streets of Dublin, many of the leaders had a second-hand memory of the Famine; some *also* had intimate connections to the old enemy. James Connolly spoke with a Scottish accent all his life. Patrick Pearse's father was English.

The Easter Rising was the formative act in the struggle for independence. 'All changed, changed utterly,' William Butler Yeats observed. 'A terrible beauty is born.' Most of the 485 victims were civilians. Forty were children.

After a two-year guerrilla war of independence, five Irishmen went to negotiate independence with the British. The fate of six counties in Ulster would remain unclear (partition remains in force at the time of writing) and politicians would have to swear an oath of loyalty to the British Crown, but the deal was done. *Most* of Ireland was free.

In December 1921, independence was granted to an Irish parliament. The terms of the Anglo-Irish Treaty would prove too moderate for a minority, though, so the nation went to war against itself for nine months of violence that traumatised large sections of society for generations to come. The Irish Civil War is often remembered with a grimace.

The Dublin-born poet William Butler Yeats won the Nobel Prize for Literature in 1923. He called it Europe's welcome to the new Free State. But many great writers, like James Joyce and Samuel Beckett, left Dublin *for* Europe. Home and away, they made Dublin a literary capital of the world.

Stuck in poverty, thousands of Dubliners voted with their feet – by emigrating. But the 1920s and 1930s were also notable for something that did *not* happen. Unlike most European countries, the state did not succumb to an extremist government of the far left or far right. Successive governments provided stability at a time of crisis in democracy.

Between 1940 and 1972, a dynamic archbishop called John Charles McQuaid doubled the footprint of the Catholic Church in Dublin, in an explosion of church- and school-building. Throughout the country, Church–state relations were cosy. Ireland was the victim and the enabler of an over-zealous parody of Catholicism.

The Irish stayed neutral in the Second World War. Coming so soon after the violent birth of the Free State, the government was determined to mind its own business. After the war, emigration and unemployment remained stubbornly high, and even after declaring itself a republic in 1949, the new Ireland continued to struggle.

In 1958, a civil servant called T.K. Whitaker told the Taoiseach (prime minister), Seán Lemass, that the national coffers were empty: it was time to open up the country to foreign investment. When President John F. Kennedy came to Dublin in 1963, the first Catholic president of the United States invited the nation to see itself anew, but also to make a society that reflected its noblest ideals.

The 1960s saw the introduction of Irish television, free secondary education, the expansion of the economy, and the launch of state-backed building schemes – including Bally-mun – that were supposed to solve the tenement problem.

In 1972, the Irish people voted to join the European Economic Community (EEC), the largest pooling of sovereignty in the history of the state. Liberal Ireland found its voice in the years ahead, and later, in the Celtic Tiger years, the economy expanded by at least 7 per cent for seven consecutive years.

The global financial crisis of 2008 revealed the shallow foundations of Dublin's prosperity, but also its resilience. At the time of writing, it is the only English-speaking capital in the European Union. The Viking town that became an English city is the Irish capital of a mature European democracy.

That's our story. Let's take a closer look at the plot.

Foundation

Geography is nature at its most capricious. Ireland is regarded as a small island because it is next door to a larger small island off the northwest coast of Europe. In the simplest and most abstruse ways, the neighbours inform our view of ourselves. But Ireland was not always an island. It was once tied to Britain.

Sixteen thousand years ago, towards the end of the last Ice Age, there was an ice bridge between the north of Ireland and Scotland. The first people who came to Ireland probably crossed from Scandinavia to Britain, and then to the north of Ireland via Scotland. Hence geography and genetics reach the same conclusion: if you go back far enough, we are all quite closely related. Perhaps we bear the same wounds.

By 12,000 BC, the ice was retreating northwards and, eventually, Ireland and Scotland were separated from each other, breaking a land route from the continent. If a nation is the same people living in the same place – as Leopold Bloom had it in *Ulysses* – this is when the Irish story begins.

The Ice Age made conditions too cold for trees to grow across much of Europe, but as ice sheets retreated, Ireland was covered in dense woodland. The first settlers probably

1

arrived about 10,000 years ago. Some historians believe that later settlers may have been attracted by reports of copper and gold, although the island had few natural resources. Today, archaeologists scour ancient rubbish dumps for scant evidence of their customs. This is not the Ireland of the Ardagh Chalice, but of flint for skinning birds and fish. The reader can still experience Stone Age life by fishing for trout.

The Eastern Triangle

Four or five thousand years ago, there were about 10,000 people living on the island. Some were the descendants of prospectors for copper and gold. Many lived in Leinster. The eastern triangle from Lough Owel to Dundalk, through Dublin, and all the way down to Greystones, is what J.H. Andrews once called 'the geographical nucleus from which men have seen their best chance of commanding the whole country'. The eastern triangle is home to Newgrange, the Book of Kells and Leinster House. This relatively small area is the cradle of Irish civilisation.

Who were these settlers? To call them Celts may be missing the point, because Celtic is a term that is more useful as a cultural marker than a defensible fact. (It entered common usage in the nineteenth century.) The word Celt comes from the Greeks, who called the tribes to their north the *Keltoi*, although there is no evidence that the Celts ever referred to themselves by that name.

Whoever the first people on the island were, we recognise their sophistication and spirituality in Newgrange, a Neolithic site that is older than Stonehenge or the Pyramids, and just as enigmatic. Never mind what you call the makers of this sacred place. We are not even sure why they built it. (Dr Pat Wallace believes the location was astronomically determined. He describes it as 'a pagan sanctuary bathed in hieratic art'.) This enigmatic monument is a source of pride and a warning from the past to the present: do not underestimate these people.

Roman Britain

In AD 43 the Roman Emperor Claudius launched an invasion of present-day England and Wales. The Romans would eventually make it to Scotland, but not to Ireland. They called the island *Hibernia*, which means 'land of winter' – a hard sell for travel agents. However, although the Romans never formally invaded, there was commercial contact, as demonstrated by archaeological finds in places such as Drumanagh in northeast Dublin and burials on Lambay Island.[1]

When the Romans abandoned Britain in AD 407, the people they left behind begged them to come back and fight the marauding natives.[2] The Romans refused, so Germanic tribes such as the Saxons and Angles came over and gradually

---

1   There is also evidence of a possible recce. Writing in the first century, the Roman historian Tacitus recounts how his father-in-law Agricola, the general who oversaw the Roman conquest of Britain, had looked across the sea to Ireland from the shores of western Scotland. He was confident that the island could be conquered by a single legion and some auxiliaries.

2   'The barbarians drive us to the sea, the sea drives us to the barbarians, between these two means of death we are either killed or drowned' – *The Groans of the Britons*.

replaced elements of the local culture. That is why the English still find Welsh incomprehensible, but they can understand bits of medieval German.

When the English (who had originally been German – keep up!) were invited to save Romano-British civilisation from the Scoti and the Picts, the south-east of England was the prized possession. The Normans (many of them were actually Norse) saw everything from France. In 1066 they pounced. So, when we look back, we remember that England is not just the country that colonised Ireland. It was a Roman province that became a colony in a French-led empire.

Christianity Comes to Ireland

Celtic Ireland was less a nation than a scattered assembly of clans and kingdoms led by chieftains and regional kings. Power was local and provisional, subject to rapidly changing fortunes. Life for most people was a dangerous and highly unpredictable privilege.

Celtic society was governed by the Brehon laws, which meant that redresses and rights were dependent on one's social standing. The intellectual elite included the hereditary poetic caste of *filí*, who were typically employed by the lords. There is evidence that women may have enjoyed freedoms that would make later generations blush, but the truth is that few people, men *or* women, lived for very long.

In the fifth century AD, Christianity arrived with Ireland's patron saint, Patrick, who was brought to the island from Britain; he is thought to have spent seven years as a slave before recovering his freedom. Today we remember him for promoting the word of God to a people who were eager to hear the good news but not prepared to forget the old ways. Thankfully, the early Christians were happy to improvise. Saint Brigid was both Celtic goddess and mother saint of Ireland. For many years, a rich vernacular religion existed alongside the Christian Church.

The date of Patrick's death, 17 March, is still a national holiday. There is no questioning his impact in a country where monasteries functioned as centres of quasi-political dynasties for many years. After the fall of the Roman Empire, they would become important places of learning, forging deep links with the continent. Indeed, Irish monks made a vital contribution to medieval Christian Europe. We know that Columbanus founded abbeys at Luxeuil in France and Bobbio in Italy. His follower, Gall, founded a hermitage in Switzerland that developed into a monastery around which the city of St Gallen flourishes. There and elsewhere, Irish monks and scribes maintained a record of Western civilisation during the Dark Ages, by copying manuscripts of Greek and Latin writers, both pagan and Christian. This was no small achievement.

The Town With Two Names

The history of a city begins when a river and a piece of land are found adequate for the needs of a people. The official account has it that Dublin was founded by the Vikings in AD 841, when they came up the River Liffey, found a black pool off

The Vikings who developed Dyflinn were 'a succession of marauding visitors'. A thousand years later, some of the people who populate the pubs of Temple Bar are not averse to the odd bit of marauding.

the Poddle, and built a ship fortress to protect their powerful longships. The original *longphort* was a defended enclosure that was designed to protect ships. A settlement emerged around it, with thatched houses on wattle paths.

Dublin has two names, which may be the earliest source of local ambivalence about the city. *Dyflinn* means 'black pool', which is derived from the Irish *Dubh Linn*. The black pool of *Dubh Linn* vanished long ago. The other name, *Baile Átha Cliath*, means town of the hurdled ford. It hardly matters that the ford was just a makeshift bridge that only half-worked at low tide. Those two titles, like a double-barrelled moniker, tell us much about a place with ideas above its station.

The leading historian of Dublin, David Dickson, calls the Vikings 'a succession of marauding visitors camping beside the Liffey'. They sound like a stag party in Temple Bar. Dickson continues: 'Initially they were perched on the edge of the shallow pool, Dubh Linn; then as they established themselves on higher ground on the ridge east of the line running from Werburgh Street to Fishamble Street, a settlement we can call Dyflyn.'

A Militarised Community

In the popular imagination, Viking Dublin sees foreigners in pointy helmets pillaging, plundering and picking their noses without bothering to look away. But the Vikings were serious people who established firm roots. By the mid-900s, Hiberno-Norse Dublin was a militarised community centred around a flotilla of long boats and a band of assertive young men.

Simple economics led to complex cultural interactions between Gael, *Gall* (Old Irish meaning 'foreigner') and *Gall-Goídil* (Old Irish meaning 'foreigner Gaels', i.e. the mixed-ethnic population of Hiberno-Norse). Trading, not raiding, became the norm; strangers settled down with Irish women, and children were typically brought up in the culture of the mother. Thor became Mick.

These Scandinavians knew how to flatter and cajole the Irish, marrying into their dynasties, allying themselves to various rulers as conflicts broke out, and establishing networks with local and overseas traders. Viking Dublin – or *Dyflinn* as it was known to them – became one of the richest port towns in western Europe and the most important urban settlement in Ireland.

Like the other port towns of Wexford and Waterford, Dublin was a magnet for immigrant settlers and native Irish. This was a place with a vibrant economic life. The Vikings traded in furs, hides, antlers and other goods; meanwhile, craftwork flourished, with wood-turning and coopering in Winetavern Street, amber- and jet-working on Fishamble Street, and leather- and bone-working in High Street.

The Vikings brought the town into a vast trading empire that stretched from the Baltic to the Middle East. They remained involved in Irish political life for three centuries, and in bloodlines for much longer: the Dublin-born reader may well have Viking DNA. Apparently a Viking athlete once caused a stir at a contest in Scandinavia when he raced barefoot – 'in the Irish manner'. (It was not just the Normans who became 'more Irish than the Irish themselves'.)

The Viking influence can be seen and heard in the Irish language, particularly in terms related to shipbuilding and seafaring, such as *accaire* ('anchor' from *akkeri*), *accarsoid* ('harbour' from *akkerissaeti*) and *bád* ('boat' from *bátr*). The linguistic influence of Old Norse is also evident in words like *sráid* ('a street' from *straeti*), *fuindeog* ('window' from *vindauga*) and *halla* ('a hall' from *höll*).

Slave Town

There are scores of Viking graves in Kilmainham and Islandbridge, where archaeologists have found weapons, tools, combs and brooches. This burial complex is thought to be the largest of its type in Europe outside Scandinavia. The grave goods discovered at these burial sites suggest that Dublin was a wealthy Viking stronghold: a place of consequence in the northern imagination. There is evidence that the maritime metropolis may also have been the sex-trafficking capital of Europe.

There were slaves in Ireland long before the Vikings. You only have to ask a primary-school student about the story of Saint Patrick, a poor teenager forcefully whisked away from his Romano-British village, Bannavem Taburniae, which may be somewhere in south-west Wales. However, while slavery existed in Ireland before the Vikings, their arrival augmented this barbaric practice.

Dublin had an active slave market between the ninth and twelfth centuries. Slaves were acquired through kidnapping, and sometimes people – often women – were sold into servitude by their own families. Business peaked in the late eleventh century, when Dublin served as an international slave-trading centre. DNA evidence suggests that many Scandinavian settlements were colonised with women who were born in Dublin. At the time, most Scandinavian families had one or two slaves.

In Iceland, a quarter of the population were Irish slaves.

The Battle of Clontarf

Legend has it that Brian Boru saved Ireland from the Vikings at the Battle of Clontarf in 1014. Looking at the teams, it was more like Leinster versus Munster. The battle saw an army led by Brian Boru fight a Hiberno-Norse alliance that included Sitric Silkenbeard, the King of Dublin and Boru's son-in-law (Sitric was married to Boru's daughter Sláine); Máel Mórda mac Murchada, King of Leinster and Sitric's uncle; and a Viking army from the Orkneys and elsewhere.[3]

There are other reasons to be sceptical about the official history.[4] Most of our information about the Battle of Clontarf comes from the 1867 translation of a twelfth-century text in Middle Irish that was commissioned by Brian Boru's great-

---

3   Confused? You ought to be. Boru was once married to Sitric's mother Gormlaith, the sister of Máel Mórda, which made Boru Sitric's former stepfather ... and Máel Mórda's former brother-in-law.

4   There is a hallucinatory strain in Irish oral history. Does this reflect the use of a powerful local stimulant? For thousands of years, magic mushrooms have encouraged storytellers to make imaginative leaps. Psilocybin may explain why the Battle of Clontarf features showers of scalding blood, angry swords and axes with the power to move all by themselves.

grandson, who just happened to be king at the time. He is a credible source in the same way that Ross O'Carroll-Kelly is an authority on rugby. It depends who you ask.

Brian Boru was victorious, but he was killed in the day-long battle, along with many of his men. He is remembered as a hero for freeing the Irish from foreign domination, but the Battle of Hastings was probably a bigger deal for Ireland in the long run. The Norman overthrow of Anglo-Saxon England led by William the Conqueror – or 'the Bastard' as he was known – would soon lead to the transformation of governance, language and customs in Ireland.

The Anglo-Norman City

By the beginning of the twelfth century, Dublin was an open, independent, Hiberno-Norse town with a flotilla of ships, its own coins and trading connections as near as the Isle of Man and as far as the Black Sea. Tensions among the ruling elite were about to have a profound effect on the town *and the rest of Ireland*. A well-to-do wobble would undermine everything.

The death of Muirchertach Mac Lochlainn, High King of Ireland, led to a power vacuum, which was filled by Ruaidrí Ua Conchobair, who came to Dublin in 1166 and was crowned King of Ireland. Ua Conchobair promptly went to war with the King of Leinster, Diarmait Mac Murchada. Some accounts tell us that Mac Murchada kidnapped Derbfhorgaill, wife of the one-eyed King Tigernán Ua Ruairc, thus upsetting the other overlords. Limited space precludes a rehearsal of the many grievances in this classic Irish feud. Just remember that it was Mac Murchada who crossed the Irish Sea in a fit of pique. In 1166, he went to ask Henry II for help to regain Leinster.

Mac Murchada found the King in France, busy attending to his own problems. Reluctant to disappoint the weary traveller, Henry II gave Mac Murchada permission to recruit soldiers from his ranks. That is how Strongbow was hired to fight as a mercenary in a proto-Irish civil war.

The exiled King of Leinster returned to England and personally enlisted the help of Strongbow, Earl of Pembroke and Strigoil. Mac Murchada offered Strongbow the hand of his daughter, Aoife, in marriage, along with the right to succeed Mac Murchada to the kingship of Leinster. In other words, this Diarmait Mac Murchada married off his daughter and gave away his kingdom (and his country) in order to advance his own position.[1]

Strongbow landed near Waterford on 23 August 1170 with a force of about 200 French-speaking knights and 1,000 troops. He went on to capture Dublin. To justify the invasion, Strongbow claimed to have a papal bull, or public decree, issued by the English Pope, Adrian IV.[2] This is where Irish history starts to sound like *The Da Vinci Code*. The mysterious papal bull gave Henry II of England the authority to invade and govern Ireland. The bull states: 'we consider it pleasing and acceptable that you should enter that island [i.e. Ireland] for the purpose of enlarging the boundaries of the Church, checking the descent of wickedness, correcting morals and implanting virtues, and encouraging the growth of the faith in Christ'.

---

1   Mac Murchada's treachery inspired a president of the United States to teach his compatriots how *not* to behave. In his book *Dermot MacMorrogh, or The Conquest of Ireland* (1832), John Quincy Adams warned fellow Americans about an example 'of a country sold to a foreign invader by the joint agency of violated marriage vows, unprincipled ambition and religious imposture'.

2   Adrian was the first and last English pope.

In 1171, Strongbow declared himself King of Leinster after the death of his father-in-law, Mac Murchada. Wary of Strongbow securing too much power, Henry II decided to affirm his ultimate sovereignty by mounting a larger invasion. Expecting resistance from his landless vassals, Henry landed with 400 ships, 4,000 men, and siege equipment. But Strongbow and the other Anglo-Normans willingly submitted to their King. (Shortly before the Irish expedition, Henry had sent four knights to kill Thomas à Becket, his own archbishop of Canterbury.)

With his vassals in check, Henry set about bringing the native Irish princes under his control. On the way from Waterford to Dublin, the King received the submissions of several Irish kings and claimed the towns of Limerick and Cork as royal demesnes. Once he got to Dublin, the King who had Frenchified England demanded that his fourth son, John, would henceforth be known as lord of Ireland. Never mind the logic. The title would stick.

Henry and his entourage spent Christmas 1171 in Dublin. A contemporary cleric, Roger of Howden, wrote that the King stayed in a post-and-wattle palace that was 'constructed wonderfully for his [i.e. Henry's] use by the nobles and richer men of Ireland'. Another observer, Gerald of Wales, wrote that when Henry held a royal feast for Christmas in Dublin with the great and the good of Ireland, he wanted everyone to eat crane, a delicacy in English high society. Gerald tells us that the Irish hated the taste but swallowed their pride … and the crane.

The fall of Hiberno-Norse Dublin came at a considerable cost. A shibboleth has it that the existing population was simply

When King Henry held a royal feast for Christmas in Dublin, he wanted everyone to eat crane's flesh. History assures us that his Irish guests abhorred the taste of crane, but swallowed their pride ... and the crane.

decanted out of the city to the north side of the river, where they settled down to create Ostman/Oxmantown. Nonsense. There's no doubt that many Norse, Irish and Hiberno-Norse families left the town for good.

Securing royal over-lordship of Ireland meant consolidating a central place, and there is no evidence that anywhere else was considered. Dublin was the prize. During that long winter in the town, Henry produced a charter for his vassals. It is extraordinary that the tiny parchment of 1171 is still in the care of Dublin City Council. The charter invites the freemen of Bristol to come and settle in Dublin and assures them that they can carry over their new civic privileges in full measure.

The invitation was accepted. Settlers from Bristol and the Severn valley came to Dublin in the coming years. But the real foundational charter was written by Henry's son John in 1192. Now addressed to Dubliners, not to the men of Bristol, it sets out the competence of the local courts, the privileges that resident merchants should enjoy over strangers, and property rights. It was John who ordered that Dublin Castle should be built as a focal point for his authority.

Social and Cultural Life in High Medieval Dublin

Dublin did not become English overnight. This was *not* a wholesale takeover. In the 1200s, the town was small enough by medieval European standards, and the following centuries saw Norman control slip away outside the town.

Still, many of the men who came as allies of Diarmait Mac Murchada stayed in Dublin, generating further waves of settlement from England, Wales and other dominions of the Angevin kings. These settlers, who were of English, Norman, Welsh and even Flemish stock, would alter the social and cultural fabric of Dublin.

The Irish and Norse languages were soon heard alongside forms of English, French, Welsh, Flemish and even Frisian (a Germanic language). By the thirteenth and fourteenth centuries, the *lingua franca* of commerce was French. By-laws were written in Norman-French, and by the year 1300, the French, English and Irish languages were commonly heard on the streets of Dublin.

Defeated by the Normans in the eleventh century, the English elite remade themselves in the image of their masters, conducting the business of the court in French and using the language at social occasions. That is why French was once spoken widely on the streets of Dublin.

The arrival of the Anglo-Normans was supposed to usher in a so-called *pax Normannica*, or Norman peace. The island and its people were pitiful to the trumpet-blowers: inferior in their customs, manners and business practices. The Anglo-Normans would not only correct the tribal anarchy of Irish society. They would unsuccessfully attempt to remake the place in the image of home.

Before the Normans came to Dublin, most people lived in simple wattle-and-daub structures, made with a woven lattice of wooden strips – wattle – daubed with a glue made from wet soil, clay, sand, animal dung and straw. They didn't know what to make of the earthwork castle – known as a motte and bailey – of the colonisers.

In the thirteenth century, these simple homes were joined by stone castles and fortifications. The reader can still see a few Anglo-Norman buildings. Swords Castle was built for the first Anglo-Norman archbishop, John Comyn, around 1200. Drimnagh Castle is the only surviving moated castle in Ireland. It was erected beside a 'crooked glen' or *Cruimghlinn* (Crumlin), hence the name of the townland.

It took the arrival of the Anglo-Normans to eradicate slavery in Ireland, having already abolished the practice in England in the early twelfth century. The Council of Armagh in 1171 rang the death knell for slavery in Ireland:

> On account of the sins of the people [i.e. the Irish], especially because at one time they were accustomed to buy Englishmen both from merchants, thieves, and pirates, here and there, and to reduce them to servitude, this trouble had come upon them by the severity of divine vengeance, so that they themselves were in turn reduced by the same people to servitude ... And so it is decreed in the said council, and declared with the public consent of all, that wherever the English are throughout the island [i.e. Ireland] they shall be freed from the bond of slavery, and shall receive the liberty they formerly had.

If this sounds like good news, it is worth noting that slavery was essentially replaced with feudalism, whereby nobles ruled the roost and peasants were obliged to give homage, labour and produce to their lords in exchange for protection and land, upon which they could farm and dwell.

On the subject of domination, it is also worth remembering that the Irish mammy is there in the background, preparing the meals, looking after the children, and subject to frequent abuse. But the mother is not the subject of lofty proclamations. She is largely written out of history.

More Irish Than the Irish Themselves

Dublin was the makeshift capital of a frontier colony, and a place apart from the rest of the island. In this sinister playground of shifting alliances, wildly different fortunes, acute danger and something approaching normality, the lines of division were never as clearly drawn as pub historians imagine.

The relationship between native and newcomer was complex, awkward and provisional: some married each other; some killed each other; while the majority simply put up with each other for the sake of an easy life. There were other inconveniences, such as the smell of the place. Human waste was dumped into a public cesspit. Animals roamed the streets looking for scraps. The odours of death prevailed.

Outside Dublin, the island was largely divided between the Gaelic dynasties that survived the Anglo-Norman invasion, and the Hiberno-Norman lordship. Just like the Vikings before them, the new Anglo-Norman settlers married Irish men and women, children from each group were fostered by the other, and linguistic and cultural expressions were traded and adopted in both communities. In time it was said that the Anglo-Normans had become more Irish than the Irish themselves: *Hiberniores Hibernis ipsis.*

Gerald FitzGerald, the 3rd Earl of Desmond (d. 1398), is an exemplar for the English who embraced Irishness because he had a *grá* for Gaelic poetry. But he was the exception rather than the rule. Moreover, some Irishmen adopted English monikers to advance in English society in Ireland.[3]

The Indefatigable City

English common law replaced the native Brehon law. By 1229, Dublin had its own mayor and an embryonic council of twenty-four chief men, jurats, to make decisions. The town was, in a full legal sense, a corporation; it had its own seal and it could sue as a legal body in the king's courts. But such privileges had to be paid for, and it is a sign of Dublin's relative economic strength that it grew so quickly. Consider the transformation in the six decades between 1170 and 1230: a great royal castle was built in stone; an organisation of traders, the guild merchant, was established; several waves of English and French settlers arrived; there was a shift from post-and-wattle Hiberno-Norse-style buildings to timber homes. Christ Church got bigger, too, and an ambitious project for St Patrick's saw it transformed into a near perfect copy of Salisbury Cathedral in Wiltshire.

Suspicion of the plebs is a recurring theme in this story. In Anglo-Norman Dublin, Irish men could hold lands as a vassal – on conditions of allegiance, in this case to the kings of England – and therefore had some local authority, but most of

---

3   Robert de Bray, who was mayor of Dublin in the 1290s, had an English name, but he had to petition King Edward I of England to be granted legal status under common law.

the native Irish lacked access to the common law system, and there was no legal redress against foul play, which made street fighting fashionable.

It is worth recalling (in the broadest of brush strokes) that England was colonised by the French, and that a hundred years later, the Anglo-Normans came to Ireland and set up shop. In other words, Dublin was the first colony *of* a colony. It was a place on the edge of the world with a go-ahead culture, and all this happened long before the invention of red tape.

The Pendulum Swings

The colonial project was full of slights and misunderstandings. It took a long time for a stuttering vision of power to emerge; even then, it was a messy business.

Dublin was the centre of an expanding Anglo-Norman colony until the middle years of the thirteenth century, when Gaelic control was reasserted in parts of Leinster, most of Ulster and north Connacht. As John Gibney has written, 'Many Irish kings reached accommodations with the new regime based in Dublin, but equally, the original conquest ran out of steam in the thirteenth century.'

Then there was the disastrous intervention of Robert the Bruce in 1317. The King of the Scots nearly got his brother to burn down Dublin: Edward Bruce made it as far as the Blanchardstown Centre. The western suburbs were destroyed as a precautionary measure to protect the town.

These were miserable times for most Irish people. Poverty, disease and a long-term shift in the European climate affected public health and agricultural output. Historian Jim Lydon once started a public lecture on medieval Dublin by shocking his audience with a story about cannibalism: according to a cleric's note in 1295, the Irish poor took bodies off the gallows and ate them.

In the bitterly cold winter of 1338–39, the Liffey froze over, allowing citizens to dance, feast and play ball on the ice. Harvest failures became all too common, and a run of bad luck concluded with bubonic plague. Nearly a third of Europeans died in the Black Death. It arrived in Dublin in the summer of 1348. Within a few months, Dublin was on its knees. A Franciscan friar in Kilkenny estimated that 14,000 people had died in Dublin alone.

The plague had a complicated impact. Society ceased to function, no parliamentary sessions were held between May 1348 and June 1350, and landlords saw rents evaporate as tenants died. However, there was an upside for some survivors, who were able to profit from labour shortages, securing higher wages and better working conditions. By the late 1300s, Dublin's population stabilised at around 6,000 people.

The parliament was originally conceived as an organ of the medieval English colony, but as early as 1460 it declared effective independence, and in 1541 Ireland was recognised as a kingdom in its own right, sharing a common sovereign with England. This experiment in dual monarchy had more semantic than material significance, but the hope that Ireland might chart its own course was planted in the native mind long before the reforms of the eighteenth century.

Put simply, many people hated the English.

Tudor Conquest

In 1492, when Christopher Columbus 'discovered' North America, a shift occurred more locally. The Atlantic crossing is when Ireland acquired a new relevance as a potential conduit between the old and new worlds. As the scholar Kevin Whelan has argued: 'The European economy, which had been Mediterranean based, is now extroverted into the Atlantic, and Ireland, almost overnight, shifts from being nowhere, on the edge, the wintry edge of Europe, to being absolutely central in terms of being the nearest point in Europe to America. So Ireland's relative location switches, and when that happens everything switches within Ireland.'

Whelan is correct in the long term, of course, but at the end of the medieval era, Chester was still Dublin's gateway to England, and its most important trading partner, with Dublin traders living there, and vice versa. Salt, coal, fine cloth and ironware were shipped from Chester in return for Irish fish, skins, furs, wool, linen and blankets. A flotilla of tiny vessels made their way across the sea from Dublin and Malahide, Howth and Dalkey.

Dublin still looked eastwards, then, and because so many traders and merchants were originally from places like Chester and Bristol, some historians have argued that the typical Dublin accent – the language of the streets and markets – must have been a soft West Country burr. Folk plays, guild pageants and the writings of Geoffrey Chaucer are typically invoked to set the scene.

Outside Dublin, the colonial project proved far less successful. By the middle of the fifteenth century, the Pale – an area of English-controlled land that once stretched from Dundalk in Louth to Dalkey in Dublin – had shrunk in size, extending only to within a few miles of the city.

In the near-vacuum left by diminished royal authority, the FitzGeralds of Maynooth – the earls of Kildare – became the most powerful force in the land, overseeing Dublin for some fifty years.[1] Their great challengers were the Butlers, the earls of Ormond. These two families had much of the clout. But the earldom of Ormond was beset by succession issues that remained unresolved until 1515. At the beginning of the sixteenth century, there was no one to challenge the power of the FitzGeralds, and the English Crown depended on their support. In Ireland, the earls of Kildare were running the show.

The Break with Rome

In military news, Henry VII defeated the forces of Richard III at the Battle of Bosworth in 1485. That result ended the Wars of the Roses in England and began the Tudor dynasty. His son,

---

1   The ancestors of the FitzGerald family had prospered in the 1400s, after becoming allied with the Yorkists, one of the warring dynastic factions in England.

Henry VIII, was a preposterous adulterer who ushered in a new state religion, and the increasing confidence of the state coincided with the growth of a distinctively English culture. The first Tudor monarchs reluctantly delegated the government of Ireland to the FitzGeralds: initially to Gearóid Mór FitzGerald, who was the richest man in Ireland at the time of his death, when the baton passed to the 9th Earl of Kildare, Gearóid Óg. Between them they dominated Irish politics for forty years – until 1519, their ascendancy pacified the hinterland of Dublin.

Among those men who helped to turn the Crown against the FitzGeralds was the Dubliner Robert Cowley, merchant, shipowner and for a while a close adviser to Gearóid Mór, who was then dismissed by Gearóid Óg, before becoming an adviser-with-a-grudge to the opposition, the Butlers.

Gearóid Óg FitzGerald had all the charisma of Donald Trump and all the modesty of Donald Trump. He was the last of the great feudal lords to dominate the lordship. In 1534, he was summoned to London and promptly imprisoned. He is said to have died 'of grief' in the Tower of London after hearing that his son Thomas was leading a rebellion against the Crown back in Ireland. Eventually, 'Silken Thomas' – or Lord Offaly, to give him his proper title – was executed for treason, along with four of his half-brothers. This assault on the house of Kildare marks the moment when the governance of Ireland became a far more pressing and more profitable concern for Henry VIII. Historians detect a formidable new element in the Dublin mix: English mercenaries. Crown servants. The brutal and intimidating forefathers of the 'Masters of Dublin'.

All this happened at a time of crisis in England, where the King was desperate for a legitimate male heir. His first wife, Katherine of Aragon, gave birth to a daughter, but no son. Ruthless and impatient, Henry tried to marry Anne Boleyn, but long negotiations to obtain papal consent to a divorce failed. Henry made the decision to break with Rome, declaring that he, not the Pope, was the head of the Church in England.

Henry's break with Rome led to the dissolution of the monasteries, which greatly enriched the King and many of his clique. That decision to dissolve religious orders and close down the monasteries was a daring asset grab. Their dissolution and sale gave Thomas Cromwell and his Irish agents – including Robert Cowley – the power to silence dissent. One of the targets in Ireland was St Mary's Abbey, which is still preserved – in part – off Capel Street. It once served as the seat of royal government and a repository for state records. (It was in the chapter house of St Mary's that 'Silken Thomas' FitzGerald renounced his allegiance to Henry VIII, thus starting his ill-fated rebellion.)

In the sixteenth century, Ireland was a place of shifting loyalties. For the constant, life could prove rewarding. In 1554, Patrick Sarsfield served a term as the mayor of Dublin. The scion of an Old English merchant family (his brother and his father also served as mayor), he is said to have run the place like a nightclub called The Patrick Sarsfield Experience. The historian Richard Stanihurst – himself the grandson of a mayor – wrote of Sarsfield's tenure:

> Over this he did at the same time protest with oath, that he spent that year in housekeeping twenty tuns of claret

While a few rich men – like Patrick Sarsfield – did well out of Dublin, many of the locals had lives of acute misery. In 1575, a plague killed 3,000 people in ninety days. The culprit was the oriental rat flea.

wine, over and above white wine, sack, malmsbury, muscadel, etc. And in very deed it was not to be marvelled; for during his Mayoralty his house was so open as commonly from five of the clock in the morning to ten at night, his buttery and cellars were with one crew or other frequented.

Plague remained a threat to the people of Dublin. In 1575, a plague killed 3,000 men, women and children in just ninety days. A hospital was built in the garden of All Hallows in Drumcondra, with guards appointed to prevent escape. The plague returned in 1603, and between 1649 and 1651 another plague wiped out half of the city's population. Although the culprit was, once again, the oriental rat flea, the reputation of its host, the rat, is unlikely to recover. In the urban imagination this supersize mouse is still synonymous with disease and pestilence.

Elizabethan Dublin

This city, as it is not in antiquity inferior to any city in Ireland, so in pleasant situation, in gorgeous buildings, in the multitude of people, in martial chivalry, in obedience and loyalty, in the abundance of wealth, in largeness of hospitality, in manners and civility it is superior to all other cities and towns in that realm. And therefore it is commonly called the Irish, or young, London.

Richard Stanihurst

By this point, it should be evident that the history of Ireland is not the same as the history of Dublin. Indeed, Ireland's ills were sometimes in stark contrast to the fortunes of its largest city. A Tudor conquest in the sixteenth century gave 'young London' a renewed prominence as the centre of a larger colony. It would mushroom in size from a population of *c.* 10,000 in 1600 to *c.* 200,000 in 1800. That jump speaks to new economic energy from the Atlantic world. It also coincides with the strengthening of English control over Ireland.

It was Henry's daughter, Elizabeth I, who ordered that the Catholic St Patrick's and Christ Church cathedrals become Protestant. The same monarch established the College of the Holy and Undivided Trinity of Queen Elizabeth near Dublin, now known simply as Trinity College. Opening in 1592, the institution soon became the intellectual centre of a privileged elite. But outside Dublin, this was no golden age. Elizabeth is widely perceived as a malign figure in Irish history.

Determined to impose her will on Ireland, and in reaction to the rebellion of the Munster earls of Desmond against English rule, Elizabeth implemented a scorched-earth policy to break the power of the 'Old English' Catholic families in the province. English and Welsh colonists were shipped into Munster; tens of thousands of Irish people were killed in the process. Here was brute-force colonialism on a vast scale. Historian John Gibney has written of 'an extraordinary contrast between the relative weakness of English rule in Ireland at the beginning of the sixteenth century and the successful conquest that had been completed a century later'. Perhaps the open-faced position is to admire the audacity of the English, to despair at some of the acts committed in their name, and to remember that the Plantation of Munster has never been celebrated in Munster.

In 1601, Hugh O'Neill, the Earl of Tyrone, coaxed Spain – England's enemy – to assist in a revolt against English rule in Ireland. But the Irish and their Spanish allies were eventually defeated in a siege at the Battle of Kinsale, thus setting the scene for a dramatic reconfiguration of power on the island.

The Elizabethan Age came to an end in 1603. Elizabeth's successor, James I, successfully united the Scottish and English crowns. Here, too, was a united Ireland under English rule for the first time. At the start of the century, the Irish peerage boasted twenty-seven members, most of whom were 'Old English' descendants of the original colonists. Only three were Protestant. By 1641, the Irish peerage had mushroomed to include ninety-two members; crucially, a third of those living in Ireland were 'New English'; by 1670, most of those peers were Protestant.

To put it simply, the old Gaelic order was finished.

In recognition of this new reality, Hugh O'Neill and his supporters set sail from Donegal for Europe in 1607. In theory they went to seek support for a new uprising, but this exodus came to represent the demise of the old order. The Flight of the Earls was also a telescopic moment in the relationship with Europe, shortening the distance with France, Spain and Italy.

The descendants of the earls enjoyed success throughout the continent. Spreading their wings – and opening doors – the Irish started to pop up all over the place, as prominent Catholic families sent their sons to study or to enlist in the armies of Catholic Europe. To this day, the personality of Dublin is heavily influenced by its relationships with Paris and

Rome. The city has always been more European than a survey of modern Irish history might suggest.

In Ulster, the land that had once been owned by its Gaelic leaders was confiscated and doled out to newcomers, who largely came from the overpopulated lowlands of Scotland. These Plantations changed the religious complexion of Ulster, giving it a Presbyterian hue. The natives did not welcome the settlers.

Rebellion

The Plantations saw Irish-owned land confiscated and given to British settlers and 'deserving' native Irish lords. Many figures within the Catholic gentry resented the new terms and conditions of life in Ireland. In October 1641, Sir Phelim O'Neill, a Catholic MP for Dungannon, captured Charlemont fort in Armagh. A putative *coup d'état*, this spark would ignite a nationwide rebellion against English rule in Ireland. Conor Maguire, 2nd Baron of Enniskillen, led a failed attempt to capture Dublin Castle.[2]

What started as an attempt by the Irish to regain their lands soon turned into a no-holds-barred affair with sectarian atrocities perpetrated across the country. Innocent civilians, including many women and children, were abused, maimed and murdered on both sides of the rebellion. A woman called Elizabeth Price recalled this scene:

---

2   One Owen Connolly alerted the authorities to the daring plan, thus securing his notoriety in Irish history.

They tooke & seised on her this deponent, and five of her Children: & above threescore more protestants at that tyme in the Church of Armagh and having stript them all of their clothes cast them all into Prison ... Capt Manus O Cane & his souldjers haveing brought or rather driven like sheepe or beasts to a Markett; those poore prisoners being about one hundred and fifteene to the bridge of Portadowne: The said Captain and Rebells then and there forced & threw all those prisoners (and amongst the rest the deponents five children by name Adam John Ann Mary and Joane Price off the bridge into the water and then and there instantly & most barbarously drowned the most of them: And those that could swym and come to the shore they either knockt them in the heads & soe after drowned them, or els shott them to death in the water.

The 1641 rebellion was a response to political developments in all three Stuart kingdoms. The painful memory of the rebellion would linger in the minds of Catholics and Protestants alike. Reprisals on both sides lasted for decades.

Across the Irish Sea, James's son, Charles I, squabbled with his own parliament and then ruled by royal decree. His subjects became exasperated, and the King was forced to recall parliament in a bid to raise more money. Frustration boiled over as Charles refused to give its members real power. Both sides armed themselves, and civil war broke out in August 1642.

Throughout the decade, there was brutal fighting, punctuated by the odd ceasefire, only for new divisions to emerge. Sectarian tension remained high in Ireland. In 1647, James Butler, the Earl of Ormond, was 'so reluctant to come to terms with Catholics', as the historian John Gibney has written, 'that he went so far as to surrender Dublin to his erstwhile parliamentarian opponents'.

After the execution of Charles I in January 1649, a confederate alliance of Catholic nobles and clergy proclaimed Charles II King of Ireland. Royalist troops were sent to Ireland. They put the Irish Confederate Catholic troops under the command of Royalist officers led by the Earl of Ormond. Their plan was to invade England and restore the monarchy. The new English Commonwealth could not afford to ignore this threat. It responded with a ruthless military campaign between 1649 and 1650 and the subsequent Cromwellian settlement of Ireland, as it became known.

He Who Must Not Be Named

The Most Hated Men in Irish History is a long list, but Oliver Cromwell tops the charts. He is the outstanding villain of Irish history. The shadow he casts over this story was described by the historian and priest John Lynch, writing in 1662: 'Cromwell, though dead for others, survives for me.'

Cromwell is regarded as a proto-democrat by some English people. In Ireland, it remains fashionable to despise this evergreen villain. When Bertie Ahern was taoiseach, he visited the then British foreign secretary, Robin Cook, who had a portrait of Cromwell on his office wall. Ahern is said to have told Cook that he wouldn't sit down until the painting

In London, Oliver Cromwell is celebrated as a proto-democrat. In Dublin, Cromwell is still regarded as a bogeyman of Irish history.

'of that murdering bastard' was removed. Cook obliged. The writer Stephen Fry said, 'It was a bit like hanging a portrait of Adolf Eichmann before the visit of the Israeli prime minister.'[3]

Civil War

The English Civil War found bloody expression in Dublin. In the summer of 1649, a combined Royalist and Confederate force gathered at Rathmines to take Dublin and deprive the Parliamentarians of a safe port. But the Parliamentarian leader Colonel Jones – helped by a snitch – launched a surprise attack on the Royalists, killing around 4,000 Royalist or Confederate soldiers and taking 2,517 prisoners. Oliver Cromwell called the battle 'an astonishing mercy, so great and seasonable that indeed we are like them that dreamed'.[4] But Cromwell's goodwill was short-lived: a few days later he issued a decree forbidding Dubliners from 'profaning, swearing, drinking [and] cursing'.

After the execution of Charles I, Cromwell was appointed as lord protector of England, Scotland and Ireland, having led an army coup to oust parliament in 1653. He was then made chief executive and head of state for life. While Cromwell lasted just over five years in the role – and he only spent nine months

---

3   In the 1970 movie, *Cromwell*, Richard Harris played the title character. As an Irish nationalist, Harris was a controversial choice for the role, though he delivered a fine performance.

4   For another perspective on this period, the historian Arran Henderson describes the Earl of Ormond as 'a truly dreadful wartime leader, meekly surrendering Dublin to the Parliamentarians, then dismally trying and failing to win it back a year or so later'.

in Ireland – his legacy is still remembered with contempt in the pubs of most Irish towns.

The civil wars and their aftermath were calamitous, killing a greater proportion of the populations of England, Scotland and – especially – Ireland than the First World War. It should be noted, however, that Cromwellian butchery was in keeping with the savagery of religious wars across Europe during the same period, and the situation was greatly exacerbated by the return of bubonic plague. Between famine, disease and war, it has been estimated that the overall mortality rate in Ireland was 15–20 per cent between 1649 and 1652.

Staying alive was no guarantee of a good time. In the 1650s, many people were transferred to Connacht from other parts of the country – hence the expression 'To Hell or to Connacht' – and their land was given to Englishmen. In these plantations, Cromwell's goal was to replenish the English stock in a country that did not appreciate how lucky it was to make his acquaintance. Here was a man who used military power to preserve the fruits of Civil War victory and national stability, commanding the confidence of both army and government.

The Cromwellian settlers who replaced the dispossessed Catholics eventually became the nucleus of what is today called the Anglo-Irish Ascendancy. In 1640, Catholics owned most of the land outside Ulster; by 1703, they owned just 14 per cent. This is the major event of the seventeenth century in Ireland. A new landed ruling class, mainly of Scottish and English origin, came to dominate life on the island, with sectarian identities – such as Catholic and Protestant – assuming more significance than any ethnic divide. The Restoration would make no substantial difference.

Restoration? Yes, eventually. Cromwell's death led to a moment of instability in England, until Charles II was invited to return, and return he did, resuming the throne in May 1660. Two years after his death, Cromwell was dug up and hanged for several hours before being decapitated. His head was impaled on a spike for over two decades outside Westminster Hall.

The Renaissance Arrives

There are many incidents of conquest, misery and revival in the story of Dublin. The most famous rebirth occurred on 27 July 1662, when James Butler, Duke of Ormond – who had been in exile with Charles II – returned to Ireland. In *Dublin 1660–1860*, Maurice Craig wrote of the Duke's return to Dublin, 'The Renaissance, in a word, had arrived in Ireland.'

Protestant Dubliners welcomed the Restoration of Charles II. The King gave the mayor of Dublin a gold chain and appointed him lord mayor of the 'young London'. During his ten-year stint in exile with the King, James Butler had visited the court of Louis XIV in Paris, where he came to appreciate how great architecture and urban planning could enhance the status of a city. He was the first man to imagine the metropolis that Dublin might become. Returning to the city of his dreams, Ormond was reinstated as lord lieutenant. Society entertained him with banquets and fireworks.

More than three centuries after his death, Ormond's legacy is still apparent in the Royal Hospital, Kilmainham; in St

James Butler, Duke of Ormond, was the first man to imagine the metropolis that Dublin might become. In 1662, Ormond was reinstated as lord lieutenant after the restoration of the Stuart monarchy.

Stephen's Green and Smithfield; and in the enclosure of the Phoenix Park. Today, most Dubliners would blanch at the thought of using the Liffey as a place for washing or defecating. It was Ormond who established a formal quay line and street on the Liffey quays, with buildings facing the river in the European manner. In such events, Dublin learns to stand with its shoulders back.

The latter years of Charles II's reign were dominated by attempts to exclude his openly Catholic brother James from the succession. James II did succeed, though, and during the six years of his reign, the government in Dublin was controlled by Richard Talbot, a veteran soldier now elevated to the dukedom of Tyrconnell. Here was another great reversal: one could almost describe it as a Catholic counter-revolution.

In Dublin, the corporation became Catholic-controlled, with a good showing of Quakers and Dissenters (Protestants who had separated from the Established Church). Some Protestants left for England, but the majority stayed put: a few in prison, most at home and desperate for news of a Williamite intervention in Ireland. Catholics were in the ascendancy for the first time since the Reformation.[5]

The philosopher and writer William Molyneux left a flattering picture of Dublin at this time. In a letter to his younger brother, who was studying in the Netherlands, Molyneux boasted: 'We are come to fine things here in Dublin, and you would wonder how our city increases sensibly in

---

5   When two vergers of Christ Church were imprisoned, the Catholic lord mayor said it was because they did not make the bells ring merrily enough for the birth of the Prince of Wales.

fair buildings, great trade, and splendour in all things – in furniture, coaches, civility and housekeeping.'

The birth of James II's male heir made a continuation of Catholic rule more likely. But the prospect of a Catholic royal dynasty would prove too great a provocation. A group of prominent English Protestants invited James's Dutch Protestant son-in-law, William of Orange – who was married to James's eldest daughter, Mary – to intervene. He duly invaded England in 1688, whereupon James fled, and William and Mary were crowned the following year. In England, this *coup d'état* is still described as the Glorious Revolution.

The joint rule of the husband-and-wife team brought some comfort to England, but in Ireland and Scotland, James's supporters had a different perspective: when William of Orange fought James II for the throne of England in 1690, the battle occurred in Meath.

Ireland was suddenly the cockpit of Europe.

The Battle of the Boyne

Driven from the throne, James decided to make Ireland the base for the recovery of his kingdom. He landed at Kinsale on Palm Sunday, 24 March 1689, and travelled to Dublin, where he stayed for over a year. Historian Peter Somerville-Large writes that 'the streets were freshly gravelled, hangings and flowers decorated every window, musicians played and soldiers lined the procession'. But not everyone was happy to see the beleaguered monarch. Maighréad Ní Mhurchadha takes up the story:

In the winter of 1689/90 when James II was resident in Dublin it emerged that traders were reluctant to supply fuel to the city for fear their goods and horses and carriages would be seized by the military for the king's service. This applied in particular to coal coming from County Kilkenny. The king was forced to issue a proclamation guaranteeing safe passage for such goods.

The Battle of the Boyne is remembered in the popular imagination as a straight fight between Protestants and Catholics. In fact, the Dutch leader – the *Protestant* William of Orange – enjoyed the support of the Hapsburg Empire *and* the Pope in a proxy battle over a larger set of disagreements on the continent. The Boyne was part of a bigger scuffle. Máire and Conor Cruise O'Brien wrote: 'In Ireland, the contending parties felt themselves to be fighting "for" and "against" the Pope, but the Pope was not in reality where he was expected to be. The fact remains an embarrassment to those on both sides who cherish simple historical pieties.'

Defeated at the Battle of the Boyne, King James fled to the home of the Earl of Tyrconnell in Dublin. Meeting Tyrconnell's wife, Frances, the King said, 'Your countrymen, madam, can run well.' Lady Tyrconnell is said to have replied, 'Not quite so well as your majesty, for I see that you have won the race.'

The so-called war of the two kings lasted another fourteen months, but Dublin largely escaped the worst of it; the west of the island suffered most deprivation and bloodshed. (The decisive battle occurred in Aughrim, County Galway, in July 1691.) The result confirmed the pre-eminence of the

After his defeat at the Battle of the Boyne, King James fled to the home of the Earl of Tyrconnell. 'Your countrymen, madam, can run well,' he told Lady Tyrconnell. 'Not quite so well as your majesty,' she replied, 'for I see that you have won the race.'

Protestant Ascendancy, whose domination of Irish society would continue for more than two centuries.

When King William rode into Dublin on Sunday, 6 July 1690, a contemporary source wrote, 'there was very great joy when we crept out of the houses and found ourselves as it were in a new world'. Another Dublin Protestant wrote, 'they ran about shouting and embracing one another and blessing God for his wonderful deliverance ... the streets were filled with crowds and shouting and the poor Roman Catholics now lying in the same terrors as we had done some days before'.

Despite rumours that Dublin would be torched by the departing Jacobites, the city emerged unscathed. Thus began a century of domestic peace, although wars between Britain and France recurred throughout, and they came very close to Dublin when French privateering vessels hovered on the skyline waiting to attack and seize merchant vessels venturing into the Irish Sea.

War is a great disrupter. Over 14,000 Jacobites, plus their families, had to leave Ireland after the Treaty of Limerick in 1691, which marked the end of the war between James and William in Ireland. ('... the poor Roman Catholics now lying in the same terrors as we had done some days before.') In the opposite direction, after the revocation of the Edict of Nantes in 1685, thousands of Protestant Huguenots came to Dublin in search of the freedom to practise their religion.[6] By

---

6   David Dickson points out that the Huguenots had a presence in Dublin long before 1700. For example, the La Touche family 'had a (private) bank nearly seventy years before they became the heavy lifters in the establishment of the (public) Bank of Ireland'.

1720, at least 5 per cent of the city's population was French-speaking.

The Huguenots did not simply make Dublin a more exotic place. They had a vastly disproportionate impact on the commerce and culture of the city. Meeting a new demand for luxury goods, the original 'refugees' (from *réfugier*, to seek refuge) excelled in crafts such as silk-weaving, goldsmithing, clock-making and sugar-baking. The Bank of Ireland was set up by a Huguenot family. D'Olier Street and Digges Lane are named after Huguenots. And Marrowbone Lane has nothing to do with cows. The street name should be Marylebone Lane, but Marylebone was mispronounced as Marrowbone in Dublin. Why? Because many Dubliners could not speak French.[7]

In the seventeenth century, Dublin Corporation (the city government) was religiously mixed, with a blend of Old English, New English and a few with Gaelic surnames. But after the consolidation of English power in 1691, religion became the gulf that divided the colonial rulers of Ireland from the native majority. And this sectarian division was deliberate.

One result of England's Glorious Revolution was an exclusively Protestant parliament in Ireland. It soon enacted a host of penal laws that restricted Catholic (and Presbyterian) clergy, worship, landowning, education and access to good jobs. Dressed up as measures to promote security, the intention of these laws was to keep the native on his knees. So, Irish

---

7   Cow Parlour in Dublin 8 has nothing to do with milking cows. The name comes from the French word *coupeur*, for the hem cutters, a trade within the weaving industry. In Dublin, *coupeur* was pronounced as cow-parlour, and so it remains.

Catholics could not buy land at a time when landed wealth was the bedrock of political and military power. They could not vote or sit in parliament. They were excluded from the bar, the bench and Trinity College, the only university on the island. A Catholic could not even own a horse worth more than five pounds. The wonder is that he was free to pick his own nose.

Again, it is useful to draw a distinction between two Irelands. The historian David Dickson says there was wide support for the penal laws among Protestant Dubliners, because the world seemed like a zero-sum game. 'The sudden and quite unexpected rebound of Catholic power under King James had demonstrated a hidden potency that the victors could only hold in check if punitive measures were introduced.'

In the 1690s, older Catholic freemen in some guilds retained their status, but recruitment into the trade guilds, the essential building block of the corporation, was denied to applicants who were not prepared to take Protestant oaths. In 1704, a formal legal barrier prevented Catholics from acquiring property.

Ormond's Royal Hospital, built in the 1680s for Irish army veterans, assumed the presence of an Irish army under the command of Dublin Castle. But from Williamite times, there was no separate Irish army command, rather a rotation of British regiments, paid for by the Irish taxpayer while they were based in Ireland, together with a minority of regiments that had strong Irish associations.[8]

---

8   Today, the Royal Irish Regiment of the British Army can trace its roots to 1689 when the Inniskilling Regiment of Foot was raised in Enniskillen by Colonel Zacharia Tiffin.

From 1697 some 12,000 men were quartered in Ireland, and purpose-built housing was required, hence the construction of the vast Royal Barracks (now Collins Barracks) between 1704 and 1708, on open ground between Oxmantown and the Phoenix Park. Many native Irish were employed in the supply and provisioning of this new social and commercial hotspot, from beer and hay to sex workers. When it opened in 1710, it was the largest barracks in Europe.

By 1700, Dublin was the second-largest city in the British Empire. Sixty thousand people called it home. Many of them were servants of the imperial project, almost everyone was complicit, and there was an unrepentant spring in the city's step. In the century to come, its population would triple, and the Hibernian Metropolis would acquire a shiny new face to reflect its burgeoning prosperity.

The Golden Age

It is hard to overstate the anti-Catholic strain in English history. In 1701, the Act of Settlement banned Catholics from the throne, ensuring the succession of Queen Mary's sister, Anne, rather than James II, his son or any other Catholic claimant. Ultimately, this brought about the Protestant Succession of the House of Hanover, in which a German-speaking regent was imported to rule Britain rather than any one of dozens of English-speaking Catholic heirs. But what has this got to do with Dublin?

Everything.

The English tried to convert the Irish to Protestantism. They largely failed. For many years, Dublin was an English stronghold, which made it a focal point of fealty *and* dissent. For example, when a statue of King William was unveiled on College Green in 1701, it became a centrepiece for the annual celebrations of admirers, who would parade around it to the faintly menacing sound of drums. The more devout wore orange cockades in their hats. But King Billy, as the statue was known, also became the subject of violent ridicule, enduring innumerable assaults before it was eventually blown to pieces in 1929 by drunk nationalists or an over-opinionated art critic – accounts vary.

During the reign of Queen Anne, from 1702 until 1714, the Duke of Marlborough won famous victories against Louis XIV of France, but the most significant political event during her time on the throne was the Act of Union with Scotland in 1707. England, Wales and Scotland were now part of a unified Great Britain.

Dublin was largely English-speaking in the seventeenth century. In the 1690s the population included a mixture of English and French, Protestant Irish and Catholic Irish migrants. But after 1700, the city began to attract more Catholics from the surrounding counties. They did the dirty work in domestic service, porterage and construction. If someone tried to sell you something on the street, they were probably Catholic. Sermons in Irish at early morning Mass became commonplace.

There was a diverse Protestant population in Dublin at the beginning of the eighteenth century, with Dissenters also – for a while – facing religious discrimination. They had a higher profile than Catholics in the first half of the century, although Catholics were probably in a majority again by 1750, three decades before the penal laws began to be relaxed. And Catholics remained disproportionately well-represented in low-status jobs. In short, they carried the weight of Dublin. The power and the capital largely remained in the hands of Protestants.

The 'Masters of Dublin' prospered in the eighteenth century. The growth of the Irish economy, built on agricultural exports, increased the gap between the haves and the have-nots; between landowning rent-seekers and large tenant farmers on the one hand, and small tenants and labourers on the other. As the century progressed, Dublin merchants began to sell more fine wines, fine silks, furs and coffee, and fewer of the textiles and practical goods that less affluent families required. By the end of the century there were twelve breweries along the River Liffey. The most successful of them was founded in 1759 by a dynamic thirty-four-year-old brewer called Arthur Guinness.

In times of harvest failure or scarcity, the rural poor descended on the city, flooding its streets. This toxic dependence on the capital is a feature throughout Irish history. The philosopher Homer Simpson called alcohol the cause of, and solution to, all life's problems. Ireland has the same relationship with Dublin.

England and Ireland

In the pubs of Dublin, colonisation is characterised as a brute unchanging molestation. But the subjugation of Ireland did not have a fixed character. In fact, the colonial project was a complex and contradictory venture, pursued by people with different agendas and loyalties in wildly different ages. Historian Ciaran Brady has summed up England's relationship with Ireland as 'repeated spasms of violence, repression and exploitation alternated with periods of attempted reconciliation, reform and development – each interrupted by longer spells of indifference, irresponsibility and neglect'.

Brady has also argued that the Irish character reflects great suffering at the hands of the English. In his account, England is not just the larger island to the east. It sounds like the neighbour from hell: 'a dominant, oppressive, exploitative, manipulative, occasionally kind and frequently neglectful close relation – a classic example of the Freudian fond abuser'.

Throughout the eighteenth century, Anglo-French conflicts had local ramifications – curtailing international trade, depressing export prices, and therefore the demand for everyday goods and services. The coming of distant war was inevitably a threat to trade at home. So, too, was English protectionism. Indeed, London's efforts to stymie Irish exports would provoke a delightful rebuke from Jonathan Swift. 'Burn everything English ... except their coal.' Who was this impudent wit?

Swift's Dublin

Jonathan Swift entered Trinity College in 1682 at the age of fourteen. In his final year he was *male* (bad) in philosophy and *negligenter* (negligent) in theology. Receiving his degree 'with special grace', Swift went to England, where he built a reputation for blistering prose. In 1713, he was appointed Dean of St Patrick's Cathedral and, being very proud of the title, frequently referred to himself in that manner. This is not to suggest that he was a flag-waving Dub.

Swift was famously ambiguous about the city of his birth, once cursing 'wretched Dublin in miserable Ireland'. The deanship was not immediately rewarding. 'I was at first horribly melancholy but it began to wear off and change to dullness.'

Jonathan Swift objected to a debased currency being imposed by the government. For his contribution to this cause, Dublin Corporation presented the Dean of St Patrick's Cathedral with the freedom of the city.

Six years later he confessed to his dear friend Vanessa, 'I am getting an ill head in this cursed town for want of exercise.' Still, staff were cheaper in Dublin than London, as was the cost of living.

As dean, Swift had a small fiefdom – five and a half acres of lanes around the Coombe – full of hungry supplicants who came to rely on him for support in times of crisis. His compassion was legendary. From a letter to another friend: 'I have the best servant in the world dying in the house, which quite disconcerts me.' That empathy with the poor would find full voice in Swift's *A Modest Proposal*, the greatest example of sustained irony in the English language. 'I have been assured by a very knowing American of my acquaintance in London, that a young healthy child well nursed is at a year old a most delicious, nourishing, and wholesome food, whether stewed, roasted, baked, or boiled; and I make no doubt that it will equally serve in a fricassee or a ragout.'

Did Swift really want people to eat their own children? No, of course not. He was mocking the government's callous treatment of the poor. When the Dean died in 1745, Dubliners filed past his coffin for two days. They knew his genius well. That gift with language, all that cranky kindness – these are *very* Dublin. In fact, the author of *Gulliver's Travels* was the city's first great celebrity. He becomes more famous and more prescient every year.[1]

---

1   Behind St Patrick's Cathedral, a housing development is adorned with carved terracotta plaques depicting scenes from *Gulliver's Travels*. The 'Good Dean' is still remembered in a part of Dublin that will always be synonymous with his genius.

Second City of the Empire

The term 'Georgian Dublin' is a recent invention. It refers to the years between 1714 and 1830, when four King Georges sat on the throne. This was a golden age for building in the city, as Dublin-based dreamers made architectural history equal to the richness of their common humanity.

To be clear, that architecture was not English or even Anglo-Dutch, like the political context from which it emerges. Georgian Dublin is part of an international uniform style that can be seen as far away as St Petersburg, marked by symmetry, balance and proportion, and based on the classical architecture of Greece and Rome. There is little English about Georgian Dublin.

In the countryside, the Irish poor would continue to endure great hardship; famine, epidemics, poor harvests and arctic winters were common in the first half of the eighteenth century. But the construction of a new parliament on College Green (it opened in 1731) and splendid thoroughfares, along with an economic boom, made Dublin a much grander place.[2]

---

2   Property was the primary source of power. However, Dr Ciaran O'Neill has recently examined the slave economy as a factor in the development of Dublin. His conclusion is unequivocal: 'There were influential Dubliners involved in the slave economy, either as secondary suppliers or importers, or (more rarely) directly engaged in the enterprise themselves as planters, traders, or re-sellers in the American South and in the Greater Caribbean. In recent years scholars have re-estimated the impact of Atlantic-trade on European economies and widened their definitions beyond the traditional and narrow focus on the slave trade itself to include transport, re-export, financial management, and supply chains. Seen in this light, Dublin's connections to the broader slave economy can be more clearly delineated, and they are more profound than we once thought.'

Rich and poor alike were attracted by the promises of the Hibernian metropolis. By the end of the century, it was the sixth-largest city in Europe, bigger than Rome or Madrid.

In Dublin's 'Augustan Age', architects like James Gandon, Thomas Cooley, Thomas Ivory and Edward Lovett Pearce imagined a grand formal city. Many of the capital's great public buildings, such as the Four Courts, the Custom House and City Hall, were built during this time. But it is the townhouse that is perhaps most emblematic of the Georgian style.

Iconic streets lined with largely uniform brick houses, featuring handsome doors framed by fanlights, give the Georgian city its character. Although the size of the houses varies, the style remains refined and tasteful, without much ornament or fuss on the outside. As V.S. Pritchett once observed, 'The tall Georgian windows, the pilastered doorways, the fine fanlights, have a family dignity unspoiled by extravagance or pomp.'

Many of the builders and craftsmen were Irish, often from Dublin itself. Inside these houses, the creation of decorative plasterwork was a local speciality, with over a hundred firms offering, at first, the Rococo style of Robert West, and later a sterner classical style; the most celebrated exponent was Michael Stapleton, who is thought to have been responsible for the ceilings in the Little Museum.

Members of Parliament, peers and other notables needed fine residences, and developers such as Luke Gardiner – who was also an MP – were more than willing to provide them, starting in Henrietta Street in the 1720s with a mansion of his own, designed by Edward Lovett Pearce. Over the next thirty years, this wide street was lined with urban palaces, each around 10,000 square feet in floor area, with magnificent staircase halls, fine reception rooms, servants' quarters, cellars and coach houses. If you wanted to make an impression on Dublin, you built or bought yourself a pile on Henrietta Street.

Gardiner was also involved in the creation of what became Rutland (now Parnell) Square, the first of Dublin's formal squares, starting with Cavendish Row. And then Dr Bartholomew Mosse managed to acquire a plot large enough to develop, in 1751, the world's first purpose-built maternity hospital, known as the Rotunda after the form of the concert hall built alongside to support it: an apt metaphor for the pregnant body. The central part of the square became fee-paying pleasure gardens, raising funds to maintain the new lying-in hospital. And the northern side was adorned by a palatial townhouse for Lord Charlemont, designed by Sir William Chambers, who was also the architect of the exquisite Casino in Marino.

Luke Gardiner was no ordinary property developer. He was a visionary planner whose greatest achievement was the creation of Sackville Street, which we now call O'Connell Street. The upper part of the street had previously been called Drogheda Street; it was developed only a few decades earlier by Henry Moore, 3rd Earl of Drogheda, a life-size peacock whose name lives on in Henry Street, Moore Street and North Earl Street. Luke Gardiner demolished the lot to make a boulevard 150 feet in breadth, with a wide tree-lined central promenade, flanked by carriageways and houses that he specified would be four storeys in height, in the Georgian style. For a time, Gardiner's Mall became the most fashionable place in town.

It would take another two decades before London acquired a street of similar dimensions in Portland Place.

Dublin became a playground for the rich, mirroring London's role as social centre for the property-owning classes. (Unlike London, Dublin had a very large military presence.) For the elite, the city was a respite from rural isolation, as well as a marriage market, site for entertainment and information zone; and when parliament was in session every second winter, it gave extra oxygen to the social season, with an endless round of masked balls, the most fashionable entertainment of the day.

The Wide Streets Commission

A hundred years before Baron Haussmann launched his 'renovation' of Paris, the Irish Parliament passed a law in 1757 to establish the Wide Streets Commission, with a mandate to create 'wide and convenient ways, streets and passages' in the city. This was both a phenomenal abuse of power by a small self-governing elite and an unqualified win for Dublin.

The Commission had its own team of surveyors and favoured architects, and they soon took bold action, pushing Parliament Street through a warren of medieval alleys to create a more direct route between Dublin Castle and the commercial district around Capel Street. Terminating the vista towards Cork Hill, but not quite on the axis, is the domed neoclassical City Hall, designed by Thomas Cooley as the Royal Exchange and built in the 1770s.

The commissioners widened Dame Street to create a better approach to the parliament on College Green, replacing its older 'Dutch Billys' with terraces of taller Georgian houses. They also created a triumvirate in Lower Sackville Street, Westmoreland and D'Olier Streets. Then came Carlisle Bridge to link it all together.

The most powerful of the commissioners was John Beresford, MP for Waterford in the Irish House of Commons and Chief Commissioner of Revenue. Beresford was a volcanic presence in Dublin for many years. Peter Somerville-Large describes him as 'a throwback to the old Elizabethan adventurers with his particular combination of energy and cruelty'.

It was Beresford's idea to relocate the Custom House from Essex Quay to a swampy site further downriver. Appointing James Gandon as architect, he told him: 'This business must be kept a profound secret, for as long as we can, to prevent clamour, until we have everything secured.' That is how Gandon, the only son of a Huguenot émigré, came to Dublin in April 1781, instead of heeding the advances of a Russian princess who wanted him to work in St Petersburg.

Beresford had good reason to be tight-lipped, as traders in Capel Street and the Liberties were horrified that a new Custom House would be built so far downriver. In a petition, they warned, 'Wherever the Seat of Trade is fixed, to that Neighbourhood the Merchants, with all their train, will in Time remove themselves.' A mob armed with saws and shovels broke down the paling around the foundations. They were led by James Napper Tandy, a prominent Dublin merchant (also, by the way, the owner of Dublin's most prominent nose). On visits to the building site, Gandon carried a sword: '[I am] determined to defend myself to the last.' The protests were in vain, and the majestic Custom House rose up on reclaimed slobland. It was finally finished in 1791 at a cost of £400,000.

The traders who protested against the construction of the new Custom House worried that it would pull Dublin's centre of gravity to the east, which it did, but this was happening anyway. In 1745, the premier peer, James FitzGerald, the 20th Earl of Kildare, decided to build an enormous neoclassical townhouse designed by Richard Cassels on a relatively isolated site facing Molesworth Street. 'They will follow me wherever I go,' he said. He was right. After he was made 1st Duke of Leinster in 1766, Kildare House became Leinster House; the same building would later house the (Royal) Dublin Society and today it is home to the Irish parliament.

The 6th Viscount Fitzwilliam of Merrion developed the 'best' quarter of Dublin; working with the Leeson estate on its margins, Merrion Street Upper was the first to emerge, before Fitzwilliam commissioned Jonathan Barker to design a layout for Merrion Square – perhaps the most impressive of Dublin's Georgian squares. In time, its residents would include Daniel O'Connell, William Butler Yeats and Sheridan Le Fanu, who wrote the world's first teenage vampire novel. (Bram Stoker's *Dracula* also has roots in the twilight fog of Georgian Dublin. Gothic writers like gloomy streets.)

The most perfectly proportioned of the Georgian squares – indeed, the only exact square – is Mountjoy Square, which was developed by Luke Gardiner's grandson, who was also called Luke. The 1st Viscount Mountjoy, he was an MP, member of the Wide Streets Commission and colonel of the Dublin Militia that suppressed the rebellion of 1798 in County Wexford. He was killed during the Battle of New Ross.

Luke Gardiner also gave his name to the long straight street leading down towards the Custom House from the hill that is crowned by the square. Either he or his grandfather is also commemorated in the name of Gardiner Row, which was developed off the north of Parnell Square, and continues as Great Denmark Street, with Belvedere House facing the hill of North Great George's Street; later, this was matched to the west of Parnell Square by the equally impressive Dominick Street Lower. About a dozen of the original houses survive today.

By the beginning of the eighteenth century, half the ships that berthed in Ireland came to Dublin, which offered the best communications between the Crown and its first colony. But navigation was bedevilled by a sand bar in Dublin Bay. In 1708 a new Ballast Office was given the power to compel ships to take sand from the river channel as ballast to help keep it clear. Its efforts would prove successful, giving local businessmen, such as Arthur Guinness, unfettered access to a larger market. (Guinness started to export his beer to England in 1769.)

The Ballast Office also built the Great South Wall, a remarkable engineering achievement (and a fine Dublin walk) that extended all the way from Ringsend to the Poolbeg Lighthouse by 1795.

Five years later, Captain William Bligh surveyed Dublin Bay. It was Bligh who recommended the construction of a wall to prevent sand building up in the harbour. He correctly predicted that sand would accumulate alongside this new barrier, which we call the North Bull Wall. The result is Bull Island, a popular refuge for Dubliners to this day. Well-remembered for this civic benison, Bligh is not so celebrated elsewhere. In 1789, his own men set him adrift on the Pacific Ocean, in the mutiny on the *Bounty*. (To be fair, Bligh was not quite as toxic as the figure portrayed by Marlon Brando in the 1962 film.)

Two long canals, linking Dublin with the River Shannon, were built by rival companies to carry passengers and freight in both directions. The Grand Canal was operational in 1790, while the Royal Canal did not reach the Shannon until 1817; its original Dublin terminus was at Broadstone, before the canal was extended to meet the Liffey at Spencer Dock.

As the Enlightenment spread across Western Europe, religious institutions began to lose their influence over everyday life. City councils sought to tidy up the public realm, adding prestige to the property of the power brokers. They created more formal open spaces and strived to keep nuisances out of sight. The grand squares supported a lifestyle based on exclusivity. Parks were reserved for the elite where promenades could yield leisure and sociability.

A Social Pyramid

A tiny elite controlled everything that mattered. They practised a form of social isolation that would be useful in a pandemic. Houses were designed for carriage transport, and while distinguished residents were sometimes seen walking the streets, a sedan chair stood in the hallways of all great houses.[3] Affluent families often kept their children at home, where they were taught by private tutors. Segregation extended to household functions, with separate stairs allowing servants to enter the house unseen.

Wealthy Dubliners wore custom-made garments, and wigs, jewellery and perfumes emphasised the good taste of the wearer. Competition between social climbers extended across all the best venues. Within the Protestant churches this contest included purchase of the best seats for Sunday services. At St Ann's church on Dawson Street, the same rich faces had the same view each week; such consistency was *à la mode* in Georgian Dublin.

For entertainment, the middle and upper classes went to the theatres, which had the thrill of being slightly risqué. Two soldiers with fixed bayonets kept punters off the stage. Shakespeare was a favourite of Dublin audiences, and inveterate theatregoers included Samuel Whyte, the schoolmaster on Grafton Street whose pupils included Richard Brinsley Sheridan, Thomas Moore, Robert Emmet and the Duke of Wellington.[4]

---

3   A sedan chair usually consisted of a seat inside a cabin with a detachable roof, mounted on two poles and carried by two men, one at each end. There were 400 public sedans for hire in 1771. For many years, sedans could be hired on the corner of Hume Street and St Stephen's Green.

4   The Duke of Wellington, Arthur Wellesley, once sat as an MP in the Irish House of Commons. After his victory at Waterloo, he was elevated to duke, and later served two rocky terms as prime minister, though he did play a key role in securing Catholic Emancipation. Some years later, Daniel O'Connell teased him, 'The poor old Duke! What shall I say of him? To be sure he was born in Ireland, but being born in a stable does not make a man a horse.'

Live music was an equally popular diversion for the well-to-do. On 13 April 1742, about 700 people attended the world premiere of George Friedrich Handel's *Messiah* at the New Music Hall on Fishamble Street. In order to accommodate as many audience members as possible, gentlemen were requested to remove their swords and ladies were asked not to wear hoops in their dresses.

Dublin was a violent and unpredictable place. The urban monsters of the day included pinkindindies: scoundrels who used a concealed sword to nip their victims. There were several hundred duels each year. Rogues like Buck English and Buck Jones were best avoided. They would push passers-by into the street and then demand satisfaction.

At the bottom of the social pyramid were the poor, who passed away a brief existence, seeking food and shelter where they might find it. Rioting was commonplace. Householders were encouraged to keep a blunderbuss handy. Kidnapping was common, too, with some of the victims as young as four years old. Public whipping was a feature of street life and one woman who tried to steal three children in Francis Street was executed, while others were thrown into the Liffey, had their ears cut off or were dragged naked through the gutter. (Hanging, prison and transportation were among the options in a criminal justice system that was overzealous and indiscriminate.) Boys and girls were often abducted by beggars. One common ploy was to disfigure the children in order to arouse compassion among alms-givers.

Visitors to Dublin noted crowds of beggars surrounding newcomers 'roaring with hunger'. This metropolis was captured

Dublin was a dangerous place in the eighteenth century. If you had money, you did everything you could to avoid the riff-raff. If you were poor, you risked life and limb every time you left your home.

in the *Cries of Dublin* (1760), a collection of street-drawings by Hugh Douglas Hamilton. Such images of street life remind us that the poor had few options, and life must have felt more contingent, with death or sickness a consistent threat from the cradle to the early grave.

James Malton and His Ideal City

The population tripled in the eighteenth century: it went from 60,000 in 1700 to nearly 200,000 in 1800, at which point 'Little London' had its own parliament, many great houses and places of genteel recreation. The attractions of *that* Dublin were captured by a young architectural draughtsman called James Malton. His twenty-five aquatint engravings are a striking group portrait of the city at the height of its Golden Age. The Englishman was not mocking the pretensions of a provincial town. He was saluting the sixth-biggest metropolis in Europe.

Malton had little time for urban squalor. He depicts the city as one of the most splendid European capitals.[5] There are broad thoroughfares lined with elegant buildings, opulent squares of red-brick terraced houses, and grand public buildings. *The Irish Times* once described his Dublin views as 'ubiquitous to the point of invisibility'. He always had an eye on the market,

---

5   Today, no artist would ignore the reality of life on our streets. But this masterful survey of the pre-Union cityscape is not just reverie. It is also a provocation to the present moment when Dubliners are self-consciously reimagining the future of the capital. Here is a panoramic urban view without cars or visual detritus. Here, too, is an Irish parliament in the natural home for such a building. If we want to build a more beautiful metropolis, we might look to the future, but also to the past.

hence the 'atmosphere of Arcadian clarity' – in Maurice Craig's phrase – throughout these engravings. But the project was a flop. It left Malton virtually broke.

The political and commercial context in which Malton had to operate is delineated in his engraving of the old parliament on College Green. As we have seen, only Protestants could become members of parliament, although Catholic men regained the right to vote in 1793 (if they owned or rented property worth £2 annually) and the parliament enjoyed more legislative independence under the 'Constitution' of 1782. Some members of the Irish parliament – including, most famously, Henry Grattan – jealously guarded that autonomy.

The first version of Malton's print has three pigs in the foreground. This ironic commentary on the inhabitants suggests a spirit of iconoclasm, but the Englishman was persuaded to clean up his act: in the final version of the 'pigs plate', the animals have disappeared. Pigs were commonplace on the streets of Dublin but associating them with an unrepresentative parliament was unwise for an artist who was trying to sell his pictures to its richest members.

Malton's view of St Stephen's Green captures the cultural fizz of Dublin. That great park is where the gentry came to perform itself in public. In the centre, there was a statue of George II, the last English king to lead his troops into battle. (English was his third language.) At that time, it was fashionable to walk up and down the north side of the Green, the 'Beaux Walk', which is the primary focus of the picture. The Beaux Walk was a marriage market, the Tinder of Georgian Dublin. Large crowds gathered to gawk at the swells. Even Jonathan Swift had a mind to write:

Dublin has always had a dating scene. In the eighteenth century, it was fashionable to parade up and down the north side of St Stephen's Green. The 'Beaux Walk' was the Tinder of Georgian Dublin.

The difference is not much between
St James's Park and Stephen's Green
And Dawson Street will serve as well
To lead you thither as Pall Mall.

That comparison with London informs and bedevils the city. In Dublin, the bigger island is never far from the top of mind. In 1764, author John Bushe laments the 'inhabitants of this metropolis, whose dress, fashions, language and diversions are all imported from London'. Among true provincials, the easiest way to denigrate Dublin is to invoke the name of London.

James Malton died in 1803. In the last five years of his life, there were two rebellions against English rule; as luck would have it, he would capture the glories of Dublin just before *and* after a period of seismic change. Malton's timing was good, and he was a talented artist, but we don't even know what he looked like. When he died of 'brain fever' at the age of thirty-eight, the hapless Englishman was unmarried and broke. All he left are the bare bones of a great Dublin drawing room.

The United Irishmen

The struggle for freedom takes many forms. Consider the case of the United Irishmen. It was founded as a sworn society by predominantly middle-class Presbyterians who were inspired by the ideals of the French Revolution (*liberté, égalité, fraternité*). They wanted to secure equal representation for all Irishmen – Protestant, Catholic and Dissenter alike – in government.

Although the society was founded in Belfast, the Dublin branch had the most clout. Its members included the likes of James Napper Tandy and the Sheares brothers. Tandy was a member of Dublin Corporation, representing the Guild of Merchants. He became a popular figure in the 1790s thanks to his denunciations of municipal corruption and his proposals to boycott English goods in retaliation for Westminster's restrictions on Irish commercial activities.

Napper Tandy was one of many Francophiles in the ranks of the United Irishmen. In 1793, when he was summonsed to appear at court on a minor charge, Tandy hotfooted it to France, where he would spend nearly five years. Meanwhile, England and France would go to war against each other.

That same year, two brothers, John and Henry Sheares, witnessed the execution of Louis XVI in Paris. On a packet ship from Calais to Dover, John Sheares started to wave a handkerchief, boasting that it was stained by the blood of the recently deceased King. When someone asked Sheares why he would do such a thing, John is alleged to have replied, 'For the love of the cause!'[6]

A young man called Daniel O'Connell was also on that boat. Bemused by the behaviour of his compatriot, O'Connell was moved to articulate the ideals of non-violent political action.

---

6 In May 1798, the Sheares brothers were found guilty of treason. It is reported that the two men stood, hand in hand, on the platform, awaiting their executions. On Bastille Day 1798, the brothers were launched into eternity. The reader can see the Sheares brothers' final resting place in the crypts of St Michan's, where a plaque reads: 'Equality: it is new strung and shall be heard' – the United Irishmen's motto.

As such, that encounter represents a division of currents in Irish history.

The Year of the French

Theobald Wolfe Tone was inspired by the ideals of the French Revolution, and he looked to the French for help in fomenting an Irish rebellion. There was more than a hint of the dreamer in this charismatic proto-republican. A few years before his ill-fated strike for Irish freedom, Tone admitted that he did not personally know any Catholics. A descendant of French Huguenot settlers, this heroic *dilettante* spent a lot of time in Paris, planning an Irish revolution, enjoying *haute cuisine*, studying French and socialising with the likes of the English-born philosopher and political thinker Thomas Paine.[7]

When Tone asked the French for help 'to break the connection with England, the never-failing source of all our political evils', they responded by sending two invasion fleets. The first of those fleets (with an impressive forty ships and 14,000 soldiers) was beaten by a storm off the coast of County Cork. The second fleet arrived too late, in the wrong place, with too few troops.

Wolfe Tone was captured by British naval forces, imprisoned and court-martialled. After being found guilty, he asked to be shot as a soldier, rather than hanged. The request was

---

7   To be fair, Tone's mother was born a Catholic, and he was secretary of the Catholic Committee in 1792, when it helped to organise a great Catholic Convention in Tailors' Hall. David Dickson describes this as 'a milestone moment in Dublin history'.

denied. Many scholars believe that he took his own life while awaiting execution.

In due course, Tone and the United Irishmen would be heroicised as the originators of physical-force nationalism. But their rebellion of 1798 also enabled the British government to consolidate power in Ireland. It was time, they argued, to abolish the Dublin parliament and rule directly from London. Enough was enough.

Tandy's Return

Napper Tandy returned to Ireland during the final days of the ill-fated rebellion in 1798. His aim was to support the Irish rebels and their French allies, who were landing on Rutland Island off the coast of Donegal. However, he quickly jumped back aboard the vessel he landed on after he learned of the French General Humbert's defeat to the British at the Battle of Ballinamuck in Longford.

Napper Tandy sailed north-east and eventually ended up in Hamburg, where the British had him arrested with a view to sending him to England. But the French consul in Hamburg demanded his release because Tandy was a French officer. This *contretemps* eventually required the intervention of one Napoleon Bonaparte, who pushed for Tandy to be released. The British dared not refuse Napoleon, due to the ongoing peace negotiations between Britain and France. The fate of a single Dubliner was thus integral to the signing of the Treaty of Amiens.

Lord Edward FitzGerald

Wolfe Tone said his goal was 'to substitute the common name of Irishmen' for 'Protestant, Catholic and Dissenter'. But instead of fomenting a revolution, the rebellion of 1798 threw Ireland's government into a state of turmoil. The Crown had a network of spies and informers across Dublin, and many of the United Irishmen had no idea that their own lawyers were in the pockets of the government.

Leonard McNally was a Dublin barrister and playwright, and a prominent member of the United Irishmen. He was also an informer. It was McNally who betrayed Lord Edward FitzGerald, one of the leaders of the United Irishmen, in 1798. Another of his victims was Robert Emmet, who led the unsuccessful 1803 rebellion; McNally also defended the Sheares brothers, who were his friends and colleagues at the bar, yet he passed secret information to the prosecution.

A member of the powerful Kildare FitzGeralds, Lord Edward FitzGerald – or *Citoyen* FitzGerald as he liked to be known – grew up on the family estate at Carton in Kildare, in Leinster House (now home of the Irish parliament) and at the stunning bathing lodge in Blackrock, Frascati. None of this encouraged a fondness for English rule in Ireland.

Despite a £1,000 reward being offered for information that would lead to FitzGerald's arrest, he evaded Crown forces on numerous occasions. But on 19 May 1798, a small force led by the town major, Henry Charles Sirr, burst into his upstairs room at 151 Thomas Street. FitzGerald refused to come quietly, killing one man with his dagger and injuring another, before Major Sirr shot him in the shoulder from point-blank range.

Citoyen FitzGerald died in his Newgate Prison cell. He is buried in a crypt in St Werburgh's, close to the pub that bears his name. Ironically, Major Sirr, the man who dealt the fatal blow to FitzGerald, is also buried in St Werburgh's. Even in the afterlife, the Crown authorities remain on the trail of Lord Edward.

The Act of Union

Ireland and England are like two cranky neighbours who never run out of slights, perceived or imagined, and often change their minds about what they really want. Today, one might want to rule the waves, while the other wants to waive the rules. Who knows what tomorrow will bring?

In any such relationship, even benign actions can have a calamitous impact. Take the Act of Union. When the prime minister, William Pitt the Younger, decided to do away with the Dublin parliament, offering the Irish 100 seats in Westminster, as well as Catholic Emancipation and greater prosperity – all as carrots for a union – he was trying to solve the Irish question. At first, the Irish MPs smelled a rat. The members of Dublin's rickety parliament rejected Pitt's offer by 109 votes to 104. There were scenes of great excitement that day in January 1799, but Pitt wasn't finished, and he came back with a better offer.

Bribery is a powerful lubricant in politics. The promise of emancipation – and the right to sit as MPs in Westminster – enticed some wealthy Catholics to support a union with Britain, while patronage, bribes and intimidation did the damage in parliament. Fifteen new peers were created; promotions were promised; Dublin Castle ran a slush fund to assist its campaign of bribery. The wheeze is surprisingly well-documented. A firelighter got four quid. The Speaker of the House, Foster, was granted an annual pension of £5,038 8s 4d. The second vote passed by 158 to 115.

One of the most egregious moments in Anglo-Irish history, the Act of Union came into effect on 1 January 1801. The historian W.E. Lecky once said that the Act was 'extorted by the most enormous corruption in the history of representative institutions'. Grattan himself lamented, 'to find a worse government ... you must go to Hell for your policy and Bedlam for your methods'.

The decision to give power to London – a decision by an Irish parliament, that is, to vote itself out of existence – was an unpopular measure that was forced through an unwilling parliament and a hostile country by the power and money of the British government. This poem was once recited by children in Dublin:

> How did they pass the Union?
> By perjury and fraud;
> By slaves who sold their land for gold,
> As Judas sold his God.

Catholics would have to wait another generation for the English to honour their promises of the late 1790s. Emancipation was blocked by George III, who argued that it would breach his coronation oath. Dubliners were bemused but not surprised.

Nineteenth-Century Dublin

The Act of Union gave power to London. It is often said that Dublin went into a long decline. That claim is overstated and unhelpful. True, there was much fitful chugging, but freedom was in the air, the penal laws were gradually being eased, and in the form of Daniel O'Connell, Catholic Dublin was about to find its voice. The story of the nineteenth-century city is more complex and more impressive than the standard telling suggests.

But first – a two-hour riot.

In July 1803, a twenty-five-year-old graduate of Trinity College, Robert Emmet, led a botched city-centre *coup d'état*. In years to come, Irish rebels would invoke the memory of a rising that spanned a few hours of a summer evening and hardly mustered an audience. Emmet became a martyr for a great cause misremembered and a famous misquoted speech from the dock.

No one knows exactly what Emmet said before his execution, but his appeal to the future would intoxicate successive generations of Irish nationalists. In one version of the speech, he has 'but one request to ask at my departure from

Many Dubliners occupied that twilight zone between work and begging. If they did not notice Robert Emmet's rebellion, it is because they had more pressing concerns.

this world – it is the charity of its silence … When my country takes her place among the nations of the earth, then, and not till then, let my epitaph be written.'

If Dubliners did not notice Robert Emmet's rebellion, it is because they had other more immediate concerns. The streets were full of people who occupied that twilight zone in which it was hard to distinguish between work and begging. Many people scraped by, singing ballads, washing down doorsteps or selling wood for fires.

In 1819, when John Fanagan opened a carpentry business in the Liberties, Dublin was in the grip of a typhus outbreak that had already killed 5,000 people. Cholera and the Great Famine would add to the ranks of the destitute. The life of Fanagan reminds us that posterity is a harsh mistress. One of Dublin's first undertakers, he worked hard to create a business that would survive him, but when he died in 1837, Fanagan was buried in an unmarked grave.

A champion of Catholic rights, Daniel O'Connell, was instrumental in the campaign to open a graveyard in the city where both Catholics and Protestants could be buried. Glasnevin Cemetery opened its gates in 1832. Today, the City of the Dead is the final resting place of over 1.5 million people. O'Connell is there, of course. So, too, are Constance Markievicz, Brendan Behan, Luke Kelly and Alfie Byrne. Glasnevin is Dublin's *memento mori*, reminding us that everything in the universe is impermanent. The only refuge is the present moment.

Once again, the popular image of a place in terminal decline requires scrutiny. Post-Union Dublin was a busy city. It remained the administrative capital of Ireland, with a separate executive and a vice-regal court. The size of the public service grew to accommodate new responsibilities, and there were myriad improvements in local government, entertainment, transport and the streetscape.

In the early years of the new century, Sackville Street became home to the handsome General Post Office (GPO) and the Nelson Pillar. Both involved architect Francis Johnston. The Pillar was a 134-foot salute to Horatio Nelson from the proud citizens of Dublin for his victory at the Battle of Trafalgar.[1] (A much-loved local landmark, the Pillar remained intact throughout the nineteenth century. In another direction, the GPO became the cradle of Irish democracy.)

Gas street lighting came to Dublin in the 1820s. By the end of that decade, the city housed the new administrative headquarters for a national police service, a national education system and a poor law system. And Dublin was still home to many doctors, lawyers, bankers, insurance brokers and teachers. In the 1820s, the gentry was estimated to consist of 200 families; in time, surgeons like Sir William Stokes and Abraham Colles would become prominent in the new social order.

In 1829, Daniel O'Connell secured Catholic Emancipation, winning the right for Catholics to sit in parliament.

---

1   The Pillar was erected in 1809, just four years after the victory it commemorates. It predates the Nelson Column in Trafalgar Square by over thirty years.

Victorian Dublin

Queen Victoria came to the throne when she was just eighteen years old. This indomitable figure ruled Britain from 1837 until her death in 1901. During that time, the administration of local government was gradually transformed in a municipal revolution. As the state deepened its reach at the local level, it formed town commissions, abolished municipal corporations, and created Poor Law unions.

Meanwhile, a succession of acts broadened the franchise, and, as a result, a new Dublin Corporation came into existence in 1841. This ratepayers' assembly was predominantly Catholic, and many councillors followed Daniel O'Connell, who was elected the first Catholic lord mayor since the Reformation. This act came to represent the capture of municipal government by the Catholic middle classes.[2]

The development of urban government led to better cleaning, paving and lighting of streets, social housing, technical education and public health. (In 1860, a fire in the Kildare Street Club was among the events that led to the creation of Dublin Fire Brigade.) Catholics secured control of much of the administrative machine for the first time, as the corporation came under the control of the Catholic and nationalist propertied classes. City Hall played a key role in advancing the politics of Home Rule and, eventually, Sinn Féin.

---

2   O'Connell did not enjoy his term as lord mayor. In a letter he moaned, 'A fortnight more and I shall have the privilege of knocking down any man who calls me My Lord.' It would be unfair for Dublin to claim O'Connell over his birthplace in Kerry.

For many Irishmen, the Royal Irish Constabulary offered a way off the land. Policemen had to be five foot eight inches tall, hence the phrase 'the tall sons of small farmers'.

While nationalists secured new powers, it should be noted that law and order remained firmly within the bailiwick of Dublin Castle. The Royal Irish Constabulary (RIC) was the police force in Ireland from 1822. Policemen had to be five foot eight inches tall, and the profession offered a respectable way off the land, leading to the phrase 'the tall sons of small farmers'. (The helmet served as a prop to make them taller still.) A separate force, the unarmed Dublin Metropolitan Police (DMP), patrolled County Dublin and parts of Wicklow. The criminal justice system reflected the moral impoverishment of the age. In the 1890s, a ten-year-old Dublin girl was sentenced to two years in prison and six years in a reformatory for stealing a prayer book.

Religious Dynamism

Catholic Ireland owes much to the imagination of Paul Cullen, archbishop of Dublin and the first Irish cardinal. Cullen was formed as a priest in the ecclesiastical hothouse of the Vatican. In Dublin he would practise a brand of Catholicism that looked to Rome for help tying its shoelaces. The ultramontane Cullen is the reason why Irish priests wear Roman collars, why they are called 'Father', and why the Catholic University of Ireland opened on St Stephen's Green in 1854.[3] As University College

---

3   Protestants were also moving into education. In 1849, St Columba's College, Ireland's first public school, moved from Meath to Whitechurch, a few miles outside Dublin. Founded to furnish the sons of the landed gentry with an education, its sister school was Radley College in Oxfordshire.

Dublin, it would eventually become the largest university in the country.

Churches were central to the reinvention of Dublin. A sort of anything-you-can-do-I-can-do-better attitude inspired Protestants and Catholics alike to build more and build bigger. Protestant landmarks had to contend with new Catholic spires, such as St Peter's in Phibsborough, with its 200-foot spire. Such projects spoke to the religiosity of the age, but also to tensions under the surface.

Much of the church-building was funded by business families, such as the Presbyterian Gothic church in Parnell Square, where Findlater money was critical; or the Unitarians in Stephen's Green, where the initial funding came from a former Bank of Ireland governor, Thomas Wilson;[4] or the reconstruction of St Patrick's Cathedral, funded by Benjamin Lee Guinness at a cost of over £110,000. Philanthropy was a competitive sport in a code that few people still play. In the 1870s, a Dublin whiskey distiller, Henry Roe, gave £230,000 to save Christ Church Cathedral. That sum is equivalent to €35 million today.

Further expressions of religious ambition and dynamism can be seen in the works of Catherine McAuley and Mary Aikenhead. McAuley founded a religious institution called the Sisters of Mercy on Baggot Street. The Sisters would go on to open free schools for the poor at a time when education was predominantly reserved for Protestants. Aikenhead was

---

4   Known as the Croesus of Dublin, Thomas Wilson was a wealthy merchant and shipping magnate. He made some of his fortune by owning 451 enslaved people.

just as enterprising. After founding the Sisters of Charity, she went on to develop St Vincent's Hospital on St Stephen's Green.[5]

The Christian Brothers also provided free education for the poor, preparing 'Paddy Stink and Mickey Mud' (as Joyce put it) for the lower reaches of the civil service, while fee-paying schools were opened by orders such as the Jesuits (Belvedere and Gonzaga Colleges) and the Holy Ghost Fathers (Blackrock College). It was not an entirely virtuous circle, for the protection of these educational interests would colour Church–state relations for many decades, and if the Church had not amassed so much power in the nineteenth century, its authority may not have been so readily abused. As Fergal Tobin once observed, 'The basic deal was church support for the politicians in return for, first, the protection of the church's educational interests under British rule, and then a controlling free-for-all after independence.'

The result of that deference to the clergy is now well documented.

Dublin and the Famine

Daniel O'Connell resisted the violent path of revolutionaries like Wolfe Tone and Robert Emmet. Today we would call him a constitutional nationalist. The force of his oratory inspired the Irish, and O'Connell was a brilliant leader, but his campaign to

---

5   The salty humour of Dublin permits no reverence. The author once heard a Dubliner talking about Mary Aikenhead in Stephen's Green. 'You know, of course, that she's the patron saint of migraines?'

repeal the Act of Union was unsuccessful, and the end of his life was overshadowed by the Famine.[6]

In 1847, when O'Connell made a last tearful speech in the House of Commons, the blight on the potato crop was descending over Ireland. 'She is in your hands,' he said, 'in your power. If you do not save her, she cannot save herself. I predict that one-fourth of her population will perish unless you come to her relief.'

Potatoes were brought to Ireland in the late sixteenth century, after the English began their conquest of the new world. By the nineteenth century, spuds were the staple food of the Irish poor. In 1845 a mysterious blight destroyed 40 per cent of the crop. Things got worse; the winter of 1846–47 was one of the coldest on record and, as the potato crop failed repeatedly, the poor became increasingly dependent on policies made in London to save their lives.

The government response was shameful: a lot of talk in the Commons; a little help to fund soup kitchens; some employment on road-building and other public works. Ireland was next door to England, ostensibly under its care, yet two governments (one headed by Liberals, the other by Conservatives) did very little as many thousands of Irish people starved to death. Charles Trevelyan, who was in charge of the relief effort, held the evangelical belief that 'the judgement of God sent the calamity to teach the Irish a lesson'. He was knighted for his labours.

---

6   When, in 1843, O'Connell called off a monster meeting in Clontarf, after the prime minister declared the meeting illegal, his reputation suffered a blow from which he would never recover. In time, a generation of young nationalists would reject the non-violent path to freedom.

The decision to leave Ireland to its own resources proved to be disastrous.[7] For victims of the Famine, death was slow, excruciatingly painful and undignified. More than a million people died and another million emigrated. In 1847 alone, a quarter of a million men, women and children left the country. The majority went to the United States, and most of those went to New York. The country's population fell from 8.2 million in 1841 to 4.4 million by 1911.

Dismayed at the indifference of his own government, the lord lieutenant of Ireland, the Earl of Clarendon, wrote to the chancellor of the exchequer in 1847: 'it is impossible that this country will get through the next eight months without aid in some shape or another from England ... Irish ingratitude may have extinguished English sympathy, and the poverty of England may be urged against further succour to Ireland, but none of these reasons will be valid against helpless starvation.'

To measure the villainy of the government, consider this thought experiment: if a million people were about to perish in Manchester, would the cabinet have done almost nothing? It is hard to escape the conclusion that racism enabled the English government to let the Irish starve to death.

For members of the Young Ireland movement, that failure to help the poor was the *casus belli* for a brief rebellion in July 1848. (It was a year of revolutions throughout Europe.) The following year, Queen Victoria landed on Irish soil for the first time. The Famine had officially been declared over

---

7   The solution to the crisis was largely left to those with a stake in Ireland, the Irish propertied classes. This was both ill-informed and mischievously inadequate.

by the government, but there was still great suffering and the workhouses were full. Victoria wrote in her diary about the cheering crowds who came out to meet her, noting the beauty of the Irish women with their dark hair and good teeth. From an editorial in the Dublin *Freeman's Journal*: 'We again ask: is it not possible to contrive some means of saving the people from this painful and lingering process of death from starvation? Do we live under a regular or responsible government?'

The Famine left a scar on the Irish psyche. This traumatic event gave Ireland a cultural memory of anguish, but it also exposed the cruelty of British politicians; and even as it traumatised several generations of Irish people, the Famine vindicated the claims of nationalism, for nothing would ever efface the memory of the British government's indifference to mass suffering.

Ireland must be free.

An Gorta Mór – The Great Hunger – made a refuge of the Hibernian metropolis, which expanded to fill its new role. The population of the city increased during and after the Famine, as many people poured in from the countryside. Some of these migrants would stay for good, lending greater variety to the urban mix.

Some of Dublin's efforts to relieve the suffering of the poor were misguided or tone deaf. When a chef called Alexis Soyer opened a soup kitchen at Croppies Acre, an audience paid to watch, as if it were a game show. The Frenchman's initiative was mocked in the press: 'Five shillings each to see the paupers feed! ... When the animals at the Zoological Gardens may be inspected at feeding time for sixpence!' The humiliation was made complete when it emerged that Soyer's soup contained just 18 pounds of meat in 100 gallons of broth, which was used to feed up to 600 people: less than one ounce of meat per serving. Everything about this culinary charade was grotesque. Famine robbed the poor of their lives and the rich of their decency.

A New Dublin

The opening of a regular train service from Westland Row to Salthill in 1834 encouraged the middle-class revolt from the city centre. Soon going all the way to Kingstown, it was the first dedicated commuter train service in the world.[8] The novelist Charles Lever classified the original commuters:

> The 8.30 train is filled with attorneys; the ways of Providence are inscrutable; it arrives safely in Dublin. With the 9.00 train comes a fresh jovial looking sort of fellow with bushy whiskers and geraniums in button holes. They are traders. 9.30 the housekeeper trains. 10 o'clock the barristers ... Fierce faces look out at the weather ... 11 o'clock the men of wit and pleasure.

Throughout the nineteenth century, the middle classes continued to leave the city centre for the fresh air, independence

---

8 To the annoyance of drivers, all five of the original level crossings are still in use. Railways may enhance a city, but they do not always beautify it. In 1891, the Loopline linked Westland Row and Amiens Street stations. Here was an act of civic vandalism, for the bridge mars the best view of the Custom House, the greatest public building in the city.

and prosperity of the new suburbs. The writer George Moore described life in the absence of the well-to-do: 'The Dublin streets stare the vacant and helpless stare of a beggar selling matches on a doorstep.'[9]

Dublin Corporation did not control the new townships such as Rathmines, and the middle-class revolt weakened the city's tax base until something of a cross-party coalition to run the city emerged in the 1850s. It was under this regime that the old Royal Exchange on Cork Hill was purchased by the corporation, allowing it to become the first truly imposing city hall.

Mount Pleasant Square in Rathmines was the last of the Georgian squares to emerge. The west side was finished in the 1830s. Here is the *rus in urbe* spirit – the countryside in the city – with squirrels and foxes in a forest, and the faint plip-plop of tennis balls. The glove-maker from Chester who developed this square, Terence Dolan, was a founder member of the Rathmines and Rathgar Township, which also oversaw the development of predominantly Protestant enclaves like Belgrave Square and Palmerston Road.[10] When the Church of the Three Patrons on Rathgar Road was built in 1862, it was primarily intended to cater for Catholic servants in the area.

---

9   The Truman Capote of his generation, Moore plundered Dublin for his novels. Dublin got revenge with a quip: 'Most men kiss and don't tell. George Moore didn't kiss and told.'

10   As the century went on, a siege mentality set in among some Protestants, who felt outnumbered and outmanoeuvred by Catholics. This manifested itself in small bigotries. Advertisements for a servant's job might invite applications from 'a native of Scotland', or even more flatly, 'persons of the Established Church'.

In *The Plough and the Stars*, Sean O'Casey has a 'Lady from Rathmines' to provide comic relief amid the ruins of Easter 1916: a southside refugee in the detritus of revolution. The Township had a real sense of itself, even down to the design of its own distinctive street lamps, and in the nineteenth century, Rathmines extended all the way to Leeson Street. That was the border with the vast Pembroke Estate, which went all the way from Merrion Square along the coast to Blackrock and inland to Dundrum. The 11th Earl of Pembroke and his successors would develop Ballsbridge with street names that salute old boys like Anglesea, Clyde, Elgin, Raglan, Shelbourne, Waterloo and – a solitary Dubliner – Wellington.[11]

Several suburbs on the northside of the city developed on the nuclei of older villages. In Clontarf, much of the land had been owned by the Vernon Estate, which derived its name from John Vernon, a quartermaster-general in Oliver Cromwell's New Model Army. Clontarf Castle was their family seat for nearly 300 years.

For Dubliners who could not afford larger Victorian houses, shrewd builders provided parlour houses of the type that now make fashionable homes in Phibsborough and Portobello. Single storey at the front, with one 'good room' of generous proportions, they have two storeys at the rear, with a kitchen downstairs and bedrooms above. These days the toilet is found inside.

---

11 The Pembroke Township was established in 1863, largely under the control of the Pembroke Estate. Cottages were built to house its workers in Ballsbridge, Booterstown, Dundrum and Ringsend.

Horses in the City

It is hard to overstate the significance of horses in the local economy at a time when cab drivers, coachmen, carters, livery stable keepers, farriers and veterinarians all made a living off these hard-working and versatile beasts. They were even used to clean the streets. In *Ulysses*, a sweeper horse cleans the road, 'rearing high a proud feathering tail' to deposit its 'three smoking globes of turds'. Artisans made saddles, whips, bridles and harnesses, while the construction of coaches was a local speciality. John Hutton and Sons stayed in business until 1925, by which time it was building bodies for motor cars off Mountjoy Square. If the reader has ever wondered why there is a Dublin Bus depot on the corner of a Georgian square, here is the answer: that Summerhill garage was home to Huttons for 140 years.

In 1861, bus driver Patrick Hardy was approaching the steep incline of Rathmines bridge when one of his horses started to rear, causing the bus to fall through the wooden railings and into the canal below. All six of his passengers died. The disaster made international headlines. *The South Australian Advertiser* assured readers that the driver was a steady Irishman 'who is said to have been perfectly sober'. The accident also led to an enduring display of public paranoia. For many years, buses would stop before crossing the bridge, allowing passengers to alight, walk across the bridge and then re-board the bus.

On 1 February 1872, the first horse-drawn tram in Ireland made a twenty-minute trip from College Green to Garville

Avenue, via Stephen's Green and – over the same bridge – Rathmines. The historian Mary Daly has written, 'On the whole trams followed housing development, rather than instituting it.' Perhaps the horse-tram's greatest contribution was to make way for electrification. At the beginning of the twentieth century, when the last horse-drawn tram on Palmerston Road was replaced by an electric tram, Dr Bethel Solomons remembered 'how modern we thought we were and at what a speed they seemed to travel'.[12]

The fancy new trams frightened their equine competition for road space; in time, horses would be advertised as 'used to electric trams'. The tramways were also used by different modes of transport, with frequent disputes between car drivers, cyclists and tram passengers. Should electric trams be faster or slower than horse traffic? The question has the makings of a great Dublin squabble.

In Defence of Pigs

Horses, cattle and pigs were once a common sight on the streets of Dublin. But in the nineteenth century, the word pig became synonymous with filth. Middle-class campaigners vowed to clean up the city, with pigs identified as a nuisance to be removed from the metropolis. There was resistance among the poor, who often kept one or more of these animals

---

12 A Renaissance man, Bethel Solomons was master of the Rotunda, an Irish rugby international and founder of the liberal Jewish synagogue in Rathgar. Little wonder that Solomons attracted the attention of Joyce. He is mentioned in *Finnegans Wake*.

Horses and pigs were a common sight. In the nineteenth century, the poor kept pigs until middle-class campaigners vowed to clean up the city, with pigs identified as a nuisance to be removed by force.

at home. Why? The historian Juliana Adelman points out that pigs did not need much space (about six square feet); they were profitable; clean; usually healthy; and pigs could be fattened with easily available foods, such as waste products from brewing, distilling, candle-making and dairying. Some were fed on slaughterhouse offal, including the meat of other pigs, and horse carcasses from the knacker's yard.

During the Famine, pig numbers dropped across much of Ireland, but the population in Dublin rose. When a family was prosecuted for keeping seven pigs in their flat, the magistrate complained, 'The odour from the place was of the most offensive nature, and disease was likely to follow.'

Reformers continued to insist that the streets of Dublin should be free from the smell of pig manure. In 1872, there were 12,000 pigs within the municipal borough. Only 4,600 remained by the end of the decade.[13] But they did not disappear altogether. Older Dubliners can still recall pigs 'flying about the streets', as the writer Deirdre Purcell once put it.[14]

---

13 In the 1970s, Éamonn MacThomáis lamented that the smell of Jacob's biscuits in Bishop Street and Mackintosh's chocolate in Kilmainham 'have all gone now, as have the smell of pig-yards in the gardens of Georgian mansions'. The last piggery in Dublin 4 closed in the mid-1990s. It was on Heytesbury Lane in Ballsbridge. But the aromas of old Dublin have not completely disappeared. Readers can still experience the barley-roasting of Guinness, the coffee in Bewleys and, of course, the whiffy Liffey.

14 In his wonderful song, 'Thank Heavens We are Living in Rathgar', the comedian Jimmy O'Dea satirised bourgeois prejudices about swine: 'In Killester they eat cockles/And those fearful things pigs' knuckles,/But you've never heard of tripe in Grosvenor Square.'

Entertainment in Victorian Dublin

Rich Dubliners drank at home or in their clubs. The first question to be asked of a newcomer was whether he was good company over claret. For the poor, there was the pub. And at first, public houses were just that – houses, typically the home of the person who produced the alcohol. Basic enough. The classic pub design only emerged in the Victorian era, with carved wood, stained and smoked glass, polished brass, intricate tiling and mosaics.

In 1829, the Irish Temperance Movement was created to fight debauchery. More than half the adult population was said to have taken the pledge. This is one of those Irish facts that must be seen to be disbelieved. One could, for example, go to Donnybrook Fair, a jamboree held on a green a mile south of Dublin towards the end of August. The purpose was to manufacture hangovers. One could also acquire a black eye.

The fair was arranged in mock thoroughfares named after Dublin streets. They were authentic in the sense that one might be mugged. Paintings by Erskine Nicol and Francis Wheatley suggest a chaotic atmosphere. There are tents and fairground rides. Vintners and hoteliers offer food and drink. Men brawl, a pig knocks over a woman, and a theatre company presents all of Shakespeare in 20 minutes. Other attractions include Zozimus the blind balladeer and a ten-foot-tall Irish giant.

Donnybrook Fair had a seductive effect on the young. Fathers and brothers were warned to keep an eye on daughters and sisters, who faced ruin if they fell pregnant. It was common

Donnybrook Fair was properly ancient, with roots dating back to 1204. In 1822, a local paper lamented that it was a place of 'sundry assaults, fibbings, cross buttocks, chancey lodgements, and ground floorings, too numerous to mention'.

for a defrocked clergyman to set himself up in a tent, and, for a small fee, to marry a couple for the night, legitimising their fleeting pleasures in the eyes of the Almighty.[15]

In Victorian Dublin, fresh air was the fashionable solution for many ills, and sea-swimming was popular among all classes. (Men swam naked.) For more genteel entertainment, one could go to the Zoological Gardens in the Phoenix Park. The third-oldest zoo in the world was built on land secured by Sir Philip Crampton, a prominent surgeon, the owner of a medical school, a pioneering anatomist and a vocal campaigner for a reliable water supply. Known as the Apollo of Dublin, Crampton is the man who decided that his city needed a rhinoceros for the summer months.

At first, most customers were gentry, but in 1840 the operators of the zoo agreed that anyone could visit for a penny on a Sunday. Over 2,000 Dubliners came every Sunday, attracted by the promise of a special day out, a glimpse of the rhino and the much lower entrance fee. Crampton boasted that visitors were 'persons of every rank and condition of life, [who] meet on terms of perfect equality'. But Dublin Zoo was an instrument of imperial policy; this fact was made explicit when Queen Victoria accepted an invitation to become its patron. It was a cunning move, for in addition to being a

---

15 The death of the fair's proprietor, John Madden, led to its demise. When a church was opened in Donnybrook on the day in 1866 when the fair would traditionally have started, the archbishop of Dublin hailed it as a victory for virtue over vice. Remnants of the fair include a chain of grocers and the word *donnybrook*, which means a heated argument in the United States, but is – strangely – unused in Dublin.

barracks town, Dublin was also a recruiting post for colonial adventurers. By 1861, over a third of the men in the British Army were Irish-born or of Irish descent. For many working-class Dubliners, fighting for the Crown in the sunshine was preferable to doing nothing at home in the rain.

Dead or alive, animals were a source of fascination in the suburbs of Dublin. Taxidermy was made fashionable by the Queen, who had a large collection of stuffed birds, and the possession of animal trophies was said to reflect a man's social status. However, if he exhibited the 'wrong' creature, it might raise questions about his breeding, and could lead to his extinction. Such were the perils of life and death in Victorian Dublin.

Reverie and Reality

When the Great Industrial Exhibition opened on the lawn of Leinster House in 1853, the money came from William Dargan, the railways tycoon. Fifteen thousand people attended the opening by Lord St Germans, the lord lieutenant. 'All hotels were packed out,' wrote Elizabeth Bowen. 'Trade boomed; everywhere was *en fete*.'

The exhibition was designed to promote a myth. The subjects documented, including chemical preparations, horological instruments and military engineering, suggest a place with a passion for innovation. Elizabeth Bowen ridiculed that assumption: 'The Great Exhibition, one must make clear, stood for Ireland's ambition rather than her accomplishment. Failing to grasp this fact, one might be perplexed by the fact that most of the exhibits come from Britain.'

Taxidermy was fashionable in Victorian Dublin. A lower-middle-class home could feature a stuffed hummingbird in the parlour. Step up the social ladder and you might find an elephant-foot umbrella stand. Souvenirs of hunting trips decorated the great houses.

The exhibition prefigured a time when Dublin's new suburbs could boast some of the best urban environments in the United Kingdom. There would also be technical innovations in brewing and electric tramways. Citizens benefitted from a railway and new technologies in food processing and alcohol production. But it was true that the Industrial Revolution largely bypassed Dublin. And although the distilleries, the breweries, the biscuit factories and the flour mills were impressive, apart from Guinness, they were not big employers.

As the middle classes fled to the suburbs, the historic core of Dublin became synonymous with social decline. By the end of the century, 20,000 families lived in one-room tenements, in a city with the worst urban adult mortality rate in the British Isles, and the fifth highest in the world. The absence of civic leadership is exemplified in the figure of Alderman Joseph Meade. In addition to serving as lord mayor on two occasions, Meade was a slum landlord and the owner of nine tenement houses on Henrietta Street. That Georgian enclave, which had once been the most fashionable address in Dublin, was now home to some of the poorest people in the United Kingdom.

Home Rule

In 1844, a future prime minister, Benjamin Disraeli, defined the Irish question:

> That dense population, in extreme distress, inhabited an island where there was an Established Church, which

was not their Church, and a territorial aristocracy the richest of whom lived in foreign capitals. Thus they had a starving population, an absentee aristocracy, and an alien Church, and, in addition, the weakest Executive in the world. That was the Irish Question.

Thirty years later, Ireland was plagued by a combination of harvest failure and agricultural depression that led farmers to fear they would lose everything, just as their parents had in the famine years of the 1840s. The farmers prepared to resist, by refusing to pay rent until times improved.

A Protestant landowner called Charles Stewart Parnell was president of the National Land League. Instrumental in securing radical land reform, Parnell led a campaign for increased tenant rights, and for a while it seemed possible that London would grant Home Rule, a limited form of independence. It became something of a political shuttlecock, as Parnell and his compatriots were sometimes able to force the political establishment to take the Irish question seriously.

In the hung parliament of 1882, Parnell held the balance of power between the Liberals and the Conservatives in Westminster, obliging the Liberal prime minister, William Gladstone, to adopt Home Rule as a policy. But that May, the newly appointed chief secretary of Ireland, Lord Frederick Cavendish, and his undersecretary, T.H. Burke, were stabbed to death while walking in the Phoenix Park. The assassinations were carried out by members of an extreme nationalist secret society, the Invincibles. There was public outrage, not least because Cavendish was the husband of William Gladstone's niece. In response the prime minister produced a combination of reform and repression.

For Parnell, the Phoenix Park murders were proof that land agitation needed to be stopped. Shifting to the struggle for Home Rule, he became wildly popular as leader of the Irish Parliamentary Party. *The Freeman's Journal* called him 'the personal embodiment of the Irish nation'. The genius of Home Rule was that it bound together the varieties of Irish nationalism. It united British and Irish politicians in the quest for an agreed settlement in Ireland; it also linked Ulster unionists and Irish nationalists.[16]

However, the cause was seriously undermined when Parnell was named in divorce proceedings brought by Captain William O'Shea against his wife – and Parnell's long-time lover – Katharine O'Shea. Parnell was ruined. The scandal-plagued leader died a year later at the age of forty-five. Over 200,000 Dubliners attended his funeral.

The grubbiness of public life had never seemed more obvious to the Irish. As the poet William Butler Yeats would later recall, 'a disillusioned and embittered Ireland turned away from parliamentary politics'.

---

16 The historian Roy Foster identifies two great missed chances in Irish history. The first was in 1800, when the promise of Catholic Emancipation 'was ruled out thanks to the opposition of King George III'. Those twenty-nine years between the Union and Catholic Emancipation in 1829 were 'suffused with bitterness'. The other great missed chance was in 1886, when Parnell, 'in the greatest speech of his life, tried to persuade the House of Commons that if they rejected giving Ireland an autonomous parliament within the United Kingdom, they would regret it in the future ... I think 1886 was probably the last moment when conceivably there could have been a United Ireland with an autonomous parliament, under the Canadian model, within the Empire'.

Another great Dublin-born writer, James Joyce, would describe himself as 'the Parnell of art'. His first known literary effort was a poem, 'Et tu, Healy', in which he rounded on all those figures who had betrayed his hero. It was written when Joyce was nine years old.

In 1893, Gladstone forced a Home Rule Bill through the House of Commons, but it was defeated in the House of Lords. Home Rule would have to wait. Squabbling and political mathematics would hamper the Irish Party for the next twenty years.

A Culture Finds Itself

In the second half of the nineteenth century, there was a kick-back against cultural homogenisation – the imposition of English culture on the Irish people – with the birth of movements such as the Gaelic Athletic Association (GAA), the Gaelic League and, in time, the Irish literary revival. In short, the Irish imagination came of age.

The GAA was formed in 1884 with a mission to wean people away from garrison games such as cricket and rugby 'and to bring them back to enjoy instead Gaelic football and hurling'. There were 114 GAA clubs in the city and county in 1888, and by 1913 the huge crowds coming by train to All-Ireland finals led the still impecunious association to buy the old city racecourse by the Royal Canal. Croke Park was a sound investment.

The notion that the Irish language could be revived as the *lingua franca* was also part of the new cultural turn. It was a fruit cocktail of enthusiasts who established the Gaelic League in 1893. Lamenting the influence of English popular literature in Ireland, the Irish-speaking Protestant Douglas Hyde warned that Ireland was becoming 'a nation of imitators, the Japanese of Western Europe'. The exquisite bad taste of all things English was repeatedly called out in public. This is how history works: someone changes the conversation, a nation finds its voice.

Reflecting on this period, it is hard to resist the conclusion that the English did not know what to do with the restive Irish, with all their demands for self-government and cultural autonomy. The rejection of their demands was enabled by a racist caricature of a people unsuited to govern themselves: 'We are here to help.'

Here is another conclusion that is hard to escape: nineteenth-century Dublin remains overlooked by the splendour of the eighteenth century and by the volcanic and more recent events of the twentieth century. It is hard to argue with a revolution, but if the reader has ever had a drink in the Long Hall, shopped in George's Street Arcade or walked the length of Dún Laoghaire pier, then he or she has worshipped at a temple of Victorian Dublin.

These places remind us of a new and dynamic form of cultural nationalism in a society that continued to privilege the Catholic Church; a place, that is, where the expression of ideas could flourish within strictly defined conditions. At the turn of the century, Dublin was calm, devout and largely loyal. Belfast was the biggest city in Ireland.

The Irish Revolution

In the spring of 1900, Dublin decided to give itself a makeover for the arrival of Queen Victoria. The corporation commissioned a mock castle at Leeson Street Bridge so that the Queen could enter through the castle gates into *her* city. In a precise calculation of the political temperature, thirty-two members of Dublin Corporation agreed that the lord mayor should formally welcome the monarch to Dublin, while twenty-two members disagreed.

Most Dubliners had no great contempt for the aging Queen, but William Butler Yeats and Maud Gonne were united in their opposition to the royal visit. The 'Famine Queen' was accused of taking 'a withered shamrock into her hand' to recruit Irish soldiers for the British Army. (At the time, Yeats was busy dreaming of uniting the aristocrats and the peasants in a poetic coalition, with shared disdain for grubby merchants. His was a gilt-framed shamrock.)

At the turn of the century, Dublin had one of the highest child mortality rates in northern Europe. Monarchs are attended by the smell of fresh paint, and Victoria did not see the worst of a city where unscrupulous landlords let dangerous tenements to large families, the legal working age was ten years old, and girls might be lucky to find work as domestic servants, but education was out of the question.

When Reverend Gilbert Mahaffy addressed a government committee on street-trading children, he presented an image of sandwich men and barefoot urchins:

> Dublin is relatively the poorest [city] in the kingdom. There is a large number of people living on the absolute verge of poverty, and if it were not for the passive type of character so largely represented among our people, there would be a regular rising in the city, for there are large numbers of people living on such small sums of money that we who know them wonder how they keep body and soul together.

The living conditions of working-class Dubliners remained deplorable for many years, with thousands of families living in one-room tenements. In 1913, a housing inquiry revealed that sixteen corporation members owned eighty-nine tenements and second-class houses.

New Blood

At the turn of the twentieth century, almost 40 per cent of the Irish-born population were living abroad, with a quarter in the United States and one in ten in Britain. But in Dublin, at least, the traffic has always been two-way. As such, its people are related to *everyone*. Fresh blood is a constant in the history of the city, which has long been more multivarious than nationalists imagine.

The first Quakers arrived in the seventeenth century after the English Civil War. Soldiers, farmers and merchants, they won a reputation for integrity and compassion. Thriving in business, dynamic members of the Religious Society of Friends went on to build successful companies like W&R Jacob and Goodbody. Thomas Pim was chairman of the first Irish railway company that built the line to Kingstown. If the reader has ever enjoyed a sticky bun in Bewleys café, he or she will know the good of Quaker Dublin.

The first Jewish settlers came to Dublin in the thirteenth century. There were only a few hundred in Dublin until the 1880s, when a new wave of Jewish immigrants arrived from the Kovno province in Lithuania. In search of a better life, these Litvaks established a community around Clanbrassil Street and Portobello; the area became known as Little Jerusalem. In 1902, James Connolly ran for election to Dublin Corporation in the Wood Quay Ward. There were so many Jews in the area that Connolly printed an election leaflet in Yiddish. By the 1940s, there were more than 5,000 Jews in Dublin.[1]

The hero of the greatest novel of the twentieth century was a half-Jewish Dubliner called Leopold Bloom. 'Think

---

1   Baila Ehrlich is an example of the lively Jewish presence in Dublin. A diminutive figure with large glasses and a cigarette hanging from her mouth, Ehrlich ran a kosher butcher shop on Clanbrassil Street that doubled as a place of refuge. 'Apparently, the cigarette smoke added to the taste of her sausages,' says Bertha Cohen, whose family had a butcher's on the same street.

you're escaping and run into yourself. Longest way round is the shortest way home.' We walk the city in the shadow of this fictional character. And some of us keep in step. Brendan Behan said, 'Other people have nationalities. The Irish and the Jews have psychoses.' For the record, the author was born in Dublin. His grandparents were a Roman Catholic, an Irish Quaker, a Scottish Presbyterian and a Lithuanian Jew. This makes him typical.

Dubliners are related to everyone.

Vivid Faces

Some of these newcomers would form part of the revolutionary generation that Roy Foster profiles in *Vivid Faces*, a secret map of radical Dublin. All sorts of liberal concerns – secularism, socialism, suffragism, vegetarianism, feminism – find a voice, often among young people from comfortable backgrounds with strong ties to Britain. Yet they had no time for the dubious values of John Bull: 'What the Revolutionary Generation objected to was not oppression, as the canon of Irish history presented it, but the fact that the British government seemed to be imposing on Ireland a grubby, materialist, collaborationist, anglicised identity.'

Foster presents pre-Rising Dublin as a place where privilege and great promise come together in the service of freedom, independence and liberty. It's a story about dazzling promise. Ideas are welcome. Here is the city at a moment of great cultural efflorescence: bohemians debate the revolution to come in student societies, over meals in vegetarian restaurants, on late nights in Gaelic League summer schools, and at radical kitchen tables in Ranelagh and the South Circular Road. The Revolutionary Generation are a rejoinder to anyone who thinks the Irish are irredeemably conservative.

Literature, language and theatre were among the passions of those 'Vivid Faces.' Many were active in the Gaelic League, which was established in 1893 to preserve the Irish language and to promote the appreciation of Celtic literature. Founder Douglas Hyde soon found a sympathetic audience, with over fifty branches in the city by 1903, and his efforts to revive the native culture coincided with those of William Butler Yeats, Lady Augusta Gregory, John Millington Synge and others who imagined a new national literature in English.

In his poetry, Yeats was a huckster for the human heart in verse of great power and elegance. (The phrase 'Vivid Faces' comes from his poem, 'Easter, 1916'.) Here was a man whose skill as an artist was complemented by his dynamism as a public intellectual. He grew up in print, making all the mistakes of his age – including falling for fascism – but his contributions to Irish literature and the state are monumental.[2]

Yeats and Lady Gregory founded the Abbey Theatre in 1904. An instrument of cultural nationalism, it would eventually

---

2   Yes, but was he good company over claret? Probably not. Oliver St John Gogarty once joked, 'Yeats has become so aristocratic that he has started evicting imaginary tenants.' An ethereal presence at the best of times, the poet was said to float through rooms. In a famous cartoon by Isa Macnie, two neighbours, Yeats and Æ (George William Russell), pass each other on the street without saying hello, because one has his chin in the sky (Yeats) and the other is staring at his own shoes. The cartoon captures the personality of a slightly cracked genius who had almost nothing of the common touch.

become the national theatre, and the first state-funded theatre in the world, playing a singular role in the life of the nation. Along the way, Yeats often encountered what he called 'the daily spite of this unmannerly town'.

The Old Age Pension

In 1909, Dubliners welcomed the introduction of the old age pension. It is not an exaggeration to say that this civic benison had a transformational effect on the lives of many people. Men and women aged seventy and above (who were living on £31 or less per year) were suddenly entitled to a payment of five shillings a week. This was a generous sum at the time, and the introduction of the pension is a social justice milestone. On Dame Street a couple in their eighties blessed 'the postmistress, the government, and the world in general'. In Kingstown, a lady loudly objected to mixing with her social inferiors in the pension queue.

The introduction of the pension prompted the most celebrated wheeze in Irish history. Many pension claimants looked surprisingly youthful. However, as it was impossible to prove, tens of thousands of Irish people aged well under seventy could not be turned down for a pension. All over the country, middle-aged chancers testified to 'eating a potato out of hand' in Famine times.

Securing a pension was, it seems, like bagging a very unusual job. To qualify for the role, you just had to pretend to be older than you really were. If your back was bent, all the better. In this way, the introduction of the old age pension made

In 1909, the government introduced a pension for people aged seventy and over. This led to the most celebrated subterfuge in Irish history.

explicit the popular will of a beleaguered nation, determined to get one over on London.

A Promise of Home Rule

For most of the decade following Parnell's death, the prospect of securing Home Rule had seemed remote, even unlikely. However, by 1912 the Irish Parliamentary Party held the balance of power in Westminster once again, and the Liberal Party had managed to curtail the clout of the House of Lords. Home Rule was on the way.

But the unionists in Ulster had other ideas. To lead them into battle they chose the one-time scourge of Oscar Wilde, a brilliant barrister called Edward Carson. The Dublin-born grandson of an Italian named Carsoni became a most effective mouthpiece for unionism.

When the unionists formed the Ulster Volunteer Force (UVF), it altered at a stroke the rules of political debate. And when 25,000 rifles and five million rounds of ammunition were brought into the north, the UVF suddenly became the best armed force in the United Kingdom, apart from the army itself. In June 1913, sixty British officers stationed in the Curragh threatened to resign their commissions if they were ordered to quell unionist force.

The Lockout

In 1913, William Martin Murphy – supported by 400 employers in the city – set out to crush Jim Larkin's Irish Transport and

General Workers' Union (ITGWU) by locking out protesting workers from their places of work.

At 9.40 a.m. on Tuesday, 26 August 1913, tramcar drivers and conductors pinned the Red Hand badge of the ITGWU to their jackets and abandoned their trams. It was a demonstration of weakness, as the trams were moving again within forty minutes. Murphy used inspectors and office staff to replace the strikers. Attacks were carried out on workers by the police and members of the Ancient Order of Hibernians, a Catholic fraternal organisation. In response, James Connolly set up the Irish Citizen Army.

On 31 August, strikers gathered on O'Connell Street to listen to Larkin speak were attacked by members of the DMP and the RIC, who injured hundreds of people in baton charges. Three people died as a result of injuries received that day, which became known as (the first) Bloody Sunday.

Life for the poor, which had been difficult enough, now became unbearable, with many relying on handouts of bread and food parcels to stay alive. Historian Padraig Yeates described the situation as 'unbridled class warfare, only mediated by a distant British government distracted by domestic problems and the home rule crisis'. By February 1914, the demoralised strikers had basically been starved back to work.

Inevitability of Partition

In November 1913, the Irish Volunteers were founded as a nationalist response to the unionist UVF. The Volunteers were soon infiltrated by the Irish Republican Brotherhood (IRB), a secret oath-bound organisation that was devoted to the creation of an independent republic.

In July 1914, the Volunteers landed some weapons in Howth. On their way back to Dublin they were intercepted by a detachment of the King's Own Scottish Borderers but largely escaped. The soldiers, jeered for their lack of success by a crowd on Bachelors Walk, opened fire and four people were killed.

Opinion in Ireland was now bitterly divided. Many people believed that the 'historical inevitability' of Home Rule was unquestionable, but unionists were determined to resist what they saw as the breakup of the United Kingdom. Since the 1880s, partitioning the country had been suggested as a way to appease the two opposing forces. Excluding some parts of Ulster from an independent Ireland eventually became more acceptable – if only as a compromise – and by 1914 there really was no alternative.

The Great War

In the summer of 1914, the government sleepwalked into a war that would claim the lives of about 750,000 British soldiers. Historian Niall Ferguson says the events of that summer were 'nothing less than the greatest error of modern history'. The assassination of Archduke Franz Ferdinand by a Slav nationalist led to the mobilisation of French, German, Russian and British troops. The world was going to war.

In the background, the Home Rule Bill was slowly making its way to the statute books. The bill became law in September 1914 with a suspension: it would be put into action 'not later than' the end of the war. Crucially, the still undefined Ulster would not be included in any Home Rule arrangement.

The Great War changed everything. Thousands of Dubliners enlisted in the early months, seduced by talk of a noble squabble that would be resolved by Christmas. In the first weeks of the war, the diarist Elsie Henry noted prophetically how the troop ships in Dublin port 'blow awful sirens every evening at 5 and 8; they sometimes sound like wailing banshees, and sometimes they roar and bellow like some devouring beast of the Apocalypse'.

By the following spring, many of those men had returned to the port as casualties, with every social and political group represented among the injured and the dead.

The First World War was an event of unparalleled slaughter. Almost 5,000 Dubliners lost their lives in this appalling conflict: ten times the number of people who were killed in the 1916 Rising. Conversely, the war also led to an improvement in the diet and life expectancy of the civilian population. Government support of the wartime economy saw wages among the poorest groups rise, while mortality rates fell as separation payments to soldiers' wives (and well-paid jobs for women in the munitions industry) saw money flow into the tenements of Dublin.

The Easter Rising

In 1915, Irish Parliamentary Party leader John Redmond reminded his supporters that the struggle over the land had been won – British rule in Ireland was neither unduly oppressive nor unrepresentative, and besides, self-government was on the way.

But history had other ideas.

The Easter Rising of 1916 was the formative act in the struggle for independence. This short-lived rebellion is best understood in the context of the First World War and the long, tortuous relationship between Dublin and London. It should also be acknowledged at the outset that the people who launched the Rising were on the far reaches of public opinion. They had no democratic mandate.

On Monday 24 April, Irish rebels issued a Proclamation on the steps of the GPO on Sackville Street (now O'Connell Street). This document was probably read aloud by Patrick Pearse to the bemusement of urchins rubbernecking at the essential moment in Irish history. Who was this Patrick Pearse?

He was an Irish hero. A propagandist who wrote mystic drivel about spilling blood for the benefit of future generations. Shy, socially inept and irrefutably brilliant, this dreamy schoolmaster convinced himself – and with his death, everyone else – that the armed rejection of British authority was an ancient and seamless endeavour, from Wolfe Tone all the way down to himself.

The Proclamation is a strikingly liberal document. Addressed to Irishmen and Irish*women*, it 'guarantees religious and civil liberty, equal rights and equal opportunities'. The rebellion was conceived with similar latitude, as a nationwide event, but its radical leadership was focused on Dublin. Some of the combatants were drawn from the disaffected young intelligentsia captured by Roy Foster in *Vivid Faces*.

As a piece of street theatre, the Rising was impressive. At Liberty Hall, passers-by asked one of the rebels, Constance Markievicz, if she was rehearsing a play for children. As an act of revolution, the Rising was less successful. German help never arrived; a rebel leader tried to call the whole thing off; the combatants didn't have enough food and water; there was no supply system in place; and the buildings seized by the rebels were chosen more for dramatic effect than military strategy.

The north city centre suffered most of the damage in a trail of destruction that took more than a decade to repair. By the end of Easter week, 485 people were dead, the vast majority of them civilians. Forty of the dead were children.

The Easter Rising was strategically inept. Dubliners jeered at the rebels as they were led through the streets, but when the British started to execute the leaders, hostility gave way to admiration. Home Rule was buried in the rubble of the GPO. The Rising made partition of the island inevitable.

Women in the Rising

In 1914, when the First World War broke out, a committee of Dublin mothers offered to knit socks for the sailors aboard the HMS *Dublin*, a gunship in the Royal Navy. Two years later, several hundred Dublin women were fighting to take the city *from* the British. The most winning of the combatants is Constance Markievicz, who was second-in-command to Michael Mallin in St Stephen's Green.

The Countess, as she was known to Dubliners, grew up in a world of privilege. The daughter of an Arctic explorer, this socialite-turned-socialist was intoxicated by the rhetoric of James Connolly. She advised her rebel sisters to 'dress suitably in short skirts and strong boots, leave your jewels in the bank

An incendiary presence, Countess Markievicz once arrived at a nationalist meeting after a ball in Dublin Castle. Asked if she enjoyed parties in Dublin Castle, the Countess replied, 'No, dear. I want to blow it up.'

and buy a revolver.' An oft-told story has her arriving at a meeting straight after a ball in Dublin Castle, still dressed in silk ballgown and diamond tiara. When a fellow nationalist asked if she liked parties with lords in Dublin Castle, she said, 'No, dear. I want to blow it up.'

At the end of the Rising, the Countess was spared from execution because she was a woman. In the urban imagination she quipped, 'I do wish you lot had the decency to shoot me.'

In December 1918, Countess Markievicz became the first woman elected to the House of Commons, although, alongside the other MPs running on the Sinn Féin ticket, she refused to take her seat. In April 1919 she was appointed as Minister for Labour in the first Dáil (parliament).

Margaret Skinnider was also inspired by Connolly's message. A teacher from Glasgow, Skinnider cycled to Dublin to fight in the Rising, where she shot several soldiers. When Skinnider was hit by a bullet, she was treated by Madeleine ffrench-Mullen, whose life partner, Dr Kathleen Lynn, was chief medical officer for the Irish Citizen Army. (Lynn taught first aid to the rebels and ferried guns into Dublin before the Rising, even storing some in her own home.)

Winifred Carney and Kathleen Clarke were just as brave – so, too, was Helena Molony, who stormed Dublin Castle. Molony hid guns in her suitcase on her way home from London, thinking that the authorities would never search the bags of an actress. She was right, though one soldier was nice enough to carry them for her. A few months later, Molony tried to dig herself out of Kilmainham Gaol with a spoon. It is not clear if they make people like this anymore.

At the end of the Rising, a nurse called Elizabeth O'Farrell was selected to go into the battlefield and deliver the rebels' surrender to the British, with only a white flag as protection. The British sent O'Farrell back to collect Patrick Pearse, as if she were a taxi driver. In a widely printed photograph of the surrender, Elizabeth O'Farrell seems to have been airbrushed out of the picture. While some historians believe that, in reality, O'Farrell did not wish to be seen standing next to Pearse, the commander-in-chief, this 'doctored' image has come to symbolise the marginal place of women in Irish history.

Aftermath

The Rising would probably have failed if the British authorities had not executed its leaders. It was the unthinking retribution of the government that swung public opinion in Ireland, elevating marginal figures into tragic heroes, none more so than Patrick Pearse and James Connolly, who had once been ridiculed as an atheistic crank from the Edinburgh slums and, at best, Jim Larkin's pale under-study. But Connolly was no buffoon. He was now revealed as prophet and martyr.[3]

On 3 May, at 3.30 a.m., Pearse was executed by firing squad. In a final letter to his mother, he wrote, 'I hope and believe that [my brother] Willie and the St Enda's boys will be all safe.' He was wrong. Willie was executed the day after Patrick.

In addition to executing the rebel leaders, the British

---

3   As Yeats put it in his poem 'Easter 1916', 'All changed, changed utterly. A terrible beauty is born.' These over-familiar words still have the power to shock us.

sent some 1,800 combatants to Frongoch in Wales; it quickly became a university for a new generation of Irish leaders.

That summer, the political establishment struggled to comprehend the scale of the losses incurred at the Battle of the Somme – 20,000 soldiers were killed on the first day alone – but it was a small-scale insurrection that came to dominate the Irish memory. Being in the GPO was a badge of honour for many years to come. *Dublin Opinion* once joked that the building needed an extension to accommodate everyone who fought there in 1916.

In the general election of December 1918, the Home Rule movement was rejected by the electorate, and Sinn Féin was triumphant. The Irish Party went into the contest with sixty-eight seats and came out with just six. It was one of the worst electoral thrashings in modern European history.[4]

More Fighting

In Brian Friel's masterpiece, *Translations*, a British soldier tells an Irish girl, 'We tend to overlook your island.' The natives sometimes force the issue. On 21 January 1919, many of the new Sinn Féin members of parliament boycotted the House of Commons and instead met in Dublin's Mansion House,

---

4   This political transformation happened in the middle of a global pandemic. The Great Flu of 1918–19 was one of the worst outbreaks of disease in history. Influenza infected as many as 800,000 Irish people, resulting in the death of over 20,000 people. In other words, the Great Flu claimed more lives in Ireland than the Easter Rising, the War of Independence and the Civil War combined.

convening what became known as the first Dáil Éireann. In response, the government imposed martial law.

That same day, two police officers were killed by the IRA in Tipperary, kickstarting the War of Independence. As the Irish Volunteers (now known as the Irish Republican Army (IRA)) waged a guerrilla war against the Crown forces, the British resorted to increasingly violent responses, which – from 1920 – were often carried out by the Black and Tans, constables recruited into the RIC as reinforcements. There were many brutal skirmishes between the IRA and the Black and Tans, who unified the many strands of Irish nationalism. Even moderate opinion was offended by the cack-handed methods of this cut-price yeomanry.

Dublin was a key theatre in the War of Independence due to its symbolic importance as the capital: heart of the woeful colonial enterprise. It was here that the IRA could most publicly challenge the British. The city was the focus of a guerrilla war, as well as the centre of the intelligence-gathering operation of revolutionary leader Michael Collins and home of the covert Sinn Féin government.

On Sunday, 21 November 1920, the IRA killed fourteen intelligence agents. That afternoon, a group of British police and military fired at a crowd attending a Gaelic football match in Croke Park, killing fourteen people. Bloody Sunday, as it became known, provoked further bloodletting in the weeks ahead, but with both sides enduring significant casualties, it became clear that the conflict would require a diplomatic solution.[5]

---

5   There were in fact three Bloody Sundays, in 1913, 1920 and 1972.

Éamon de Valera was one of the few rebel leaders in the Rising to escape execution. A gift for avoiding disaster would prove useful in a political career that lasted over five decades. By 1921, Dev was president of the Irish government-in-waiting. It was he who sent Arthur Griffith, Michael Collins and three other men to negotiate an agreement with the British.

A charismatic military leader, Collins was reluctant to go to London and aware that de Valera might soon be looking for people to blame, but he was still prepared to make the case for the Irish. 'Let them make a scapegoat or anything they wish of me. We have accepted the situation, as it is, and someone must go.'

The Anglo-Irish Treaty was agreed at 2.20 a.m. on 6 December 1921. The negotiators knew that it would not be welcomed by all. Once again, Michael Collins had his eye on history: 'Think what have I got for Ireland ... something which she has wanted these past 700 years, will anyone be satisfied with this bargain, will anyone? I tell you this, early this morning I have signed my death warrant.'

Architects of Freedom

Returning to Dublin, the negotiators presented their deal to a war-weary public. The great public intellectual Arthur Griffith said the Treaty would lay the foundation of peace and friendship between the neighbouring islands. Michael Collins described the Treaty as a stepping stone, providing the freedom to achieve freedom, and most of his compatriots accepted that characterisation. However, some nationalists said the deal had been signed under duress – with a British threat of 'immediate and terrible war' – and that it was a form of surrender.

Under the terms of the Treaty, the Free State would remain in the British Empire, and members of the new parliament would have to swear an oath of allegiance to the king or queen. Nonetheless, the Treaty was a historic achievement, securing independence for twenty-six of the thirty-two counties on the island – and in that sense, it reflected the facts on the ground, as Ireland had already been partitioned in 1920.

Collins pushed the Treaty through the Dáil, and the Irish people overwhelmingly ratified it in the election of June 1922, when the anti-Treaty side received just 21.8 per cent of the vote. However, some republicans were unwilling to accept the result. Éamon de Valera led his supporters out of the Dáil, and the country went to war against itself. In the short, brutal Irish Civil War, nearly 2,000 Irish men and women lost their lives.

The two architects of Irish freedom did not live long enough to enjoy that freedom. Both men died just a few months after the foundation of the state. Arthur Griffith died of heart failure at the age of fifty-one in August 1922. Ten days later, Michael Collins was assassinated by anti-Treaty forces. He was thirty-one years old.

Civil War

In the spring of 1922, an anti-Treaty IRA garrison occupied the Four Courts building. When the troops of the new Irish Free State army attacked the garrison, fighting soon spread to the centre of the city, with anti-Treaty forces occupying parts of O'Connell Street, Gardiner Street, Parnell Street and Aungier Street. The anti-Treaty forces were defeated by the new Irish army after a week of heavy bombardment and street fighting. More than 300 combatants were killed or wounded, and over 200 civilians were killed during the Battle of Dublin.

The defeat of the anti-Treaty forces in the capital shifted attention to places outside Dublin, but the city remained politically contested, as the guerrilla war that followed became a vicious cycle of execution, outrage and revenge. In total, seventy-seven opponents of the Treaty were executed by the Free State government.

In May 1923, the Civil War ended in the defeat of those republicans who had opposed the Treaty, but the wounds of this conflict remained raw for decades to come. Even today, a hundred years later, many Irish people have inherited their political allegiance from a generation that was conditioned to love or hate de Valera.

The historian Margaret MacMillan has observed that the reason why civil wars are so fractious is because they are inevitably personal. 'The other side is seen as having betrayed the community by refusing to agree to shared values and a common vision and so extremes of violence and cruelty become permissible, even necessary, to restore the damaged polity.' Between 1922 and 1948, two men headed the Irish government: W.T. Cosgrave and Éamon de Valera. The bitterness between these one-time comrades was earnest and unyielding. For the rest of his life, outside the Dáil, Cosgrave refused to be in the same room as de Valera.

The Irish Civil War lasted about a year. It was a short, miserable chapter in the national story. As usual, most of the damage was done in Dublin. It is not an exaggeration to say that the capital limped into independence.

Free State Capital

Ireland was one of the first dominoes to fall during the process of British decolonisation. The creation of the Irish Free State was celebrated all over the world. After defeating the opponents of the Treaty in a bitter, short and bloody Civil War, the new regime set to work under its first leader, W.T. Cosgrave. They rebuilt the Four Courts. They decided that Dáil Éireann would sit in Leinster House, in a lecture hall provided by the Royal Dublin Society. (It was supposed to be a temporary solution.) The Dublin Metropolitan Police was amalgamated with *An Garda Síochána*. A public telephone was installed on Dawson Street. Red postboxes were painted green. The study of Irish was made compulsory in schools. And Dublin's nationalist heritage was privileged wherever possible. So Albert Quay became Wolfe Tone Quay, while the much-attacked centre of the city, Sackville Street, became O'Connell Street.[1] Fifteen

---

1   Queen Victoria still crowns a street and a quay on the Liffey, while Clontarf, Dalkey and Rathgar all have a Victoria Road. Some years ago, a hooligan daubed paint across the English version of Victoria's name on a street sign but neglected to deface the Irish translation. Such illiteracy is not normally a laughing matter.

years later, a journalist, Stephen Gwynn, wrote, 'There are still people who say "Sackville Street" on principle, and some who prefer it for euphony.'

Changing the name of a street is easier than creating a new society. The exercise was probably good for some panjandrum's ego, but the truth is that independence had little immediate effect on the lives of most Dubliners. The first government was fiscally conservative, cash-strapped and loudly Catholic.

Church and State

W.T. Cosgrave was never accused of excessive dynamism. As a devout Roman Catholic and daily communicant, he led the country in partnership with a higher power, bringing pious attention to the problems of the Free State.

Quick wins included closing all pubs between 2.30 p.m. and 3.30 p.m. on weekdays to force observance of a 'holy hour' of Eucharistic Adoration.[2] The holy hour quickly became the most joyfully ignored piece of legislation in Irish history, as patrons and publicans bent, broke and wilfully misinterpreted the ruling in search of a drink.

Absorbed by its own reflection, the state turned inward, deciding to ban any movies or books that might upset the delicate Irish mind. The first censor, James Montgomery, personally banned over 1,800 films. Calling himself a 'moral

---

2   The holy hour restrictions were lifted in 1971 with the exception of Dublin and Cork, which maintained the observance of the holy hour until 1988. A Sunday holy hour, observed from 2 p.m. to 4 p.m., was retained until the year 2000.

The writer Seán Ó Faoláin once described Catholic Ireland as a dreary Eden. The pubs of Dublin were closed between 2.30 p.m. and 3.30 p.m. on weekdays, while any movies or books that might upset the delicate Irish mind were banned or subject to radical revisions.

sieve', he cut any scenes with kissing, blasphemy, incest, divorce, contraception, abortion, homosexuality, adultery or illegitimacy. He didn't like the word virgin, or any mention of prostitutes, 'with or without a heart of gold'. Of one film scene he wrote: 'The girl dancing on the village green shows more leg than I've seen on any village green in Ireland. Better amputate them.'

In theory, public opinion would be disgusted by such scenes, but going to the movies would change the way Irish people saw themselves and the world. One of the effects was an increased appetite for film itself. By the 1950s, Dublin had more cinema seats per head of population than any other city in Europe.[3]

Prostitution and Protestantism were both regarded as toxic influences. In 1925, the Monto red-light district was shut down overnight. Three years later, the archbishop of Dublin wrote a letter on the subject of Trinity College, which Catholics were banned from attending because it was perceived as a Protestant university. As an old rhyme has it,

> Young men may loot, perjure and shoot,
> and even have carnal knowledge,
> but however depraved
> their souls will be saved,
> if they don't go to Trinity College.

---

3   Entertainments continued to be cut, censored or banned. Even classic films were so mangled by the censor that they made no sense to Irish people. The reader may remember *Casablanca* with Ingrid Bergman, Humphrey Bogart and a shameful hint of adultery? *Casablanca* made it to Ireland, but the plot did not survive the journey.

The austerity of Irish Catholicism is epitomised in the figure of Matt Talbot. A Dublin labourer who pledged to abstain from alcohol at the age of twenty-eight, Talbot maintained this pledge for forty-one years, attending daily Mass and sleeping on a wooden board. After his death in 1925, it was discovered that he was wearing chains and cords around his waist, arms and legs as a symbol of his devotion to Mary, Mother of God. He became an icon of the temperance movement.

How Are Things in the Corpo?

Clearing the slums was a litmus test for the value of independence, demonstrating that an Irish government could underwrite its own future. But this vast building project was controlled from the very centre of the establishment, within a shiny new department. Dublin Corporation – or the Corpo – was regarded with suspicion by the government as a corrupt bolthole for anti-Treaty republicans.

A corruption scandal was the pretext for a shake-up. It was alleged that some councillors had misallocated homes in a housing scheme. In the 1920s, Dublin Corporation was suspended for six years, its functions exercised by three very able commissioners. The sky did not fall in. The commissioners had a flair for public relations and boosting civic pride. They produced civic weeks and published handsome booklets, promoting Dublin as a capital of history and hospitality.

Among the many modest advances in the early years of the Free State, none improved the lives of Dubliners in the way that the arrival of the old-age pension had done under

British rule in 1909. When the government was forced to take a shilling off the pension in 1924 – money was simply too tight – the decision hit the poor hardest.

De Valera in Power

In 1932, a few days after a general election, W.T. Cosgrave accepted defeat and ceded power to Éamon de Valera and his minority Fianna Fáil government. A signal event in Irish history, this peaceful transfer of power is not remembered with any fanfare in Ireland. Taking democracy for granted: this only happens in placid states. Independence enabled splendid isolation from the wars that have ravaged most of Europe in the last 100 years.

To hand power to his Civil War enemies, less than ten years after the end of that war, was a personal defeat for Cosgrave, who would never get into power again, but it was a major achievement for a fledgling democracy. Indeed, the country *never* succumbed to a party of the far right or far left during the interwar years, in contrast to most of the new democracies in Europe, where strongmen dictators became the norm. Protecting liberty in a crisis is not the sexiest thing in the world, but the event is worth remembering.

That summer, Dev completed a remarkable comeback when he hosted the Eucharistic Congress in Dublin. Ten years earlier, he had been excommunicated by the Catholic Church, along with the other anti-Treaty leaders. Now he was presiding over the largest religious event in Irish history.

A quarter of the Irish population attended a Mass in the

Phoenix Park during the Eucharistic Congress. In a seamless joining of pious Catholicism and triumphant nationalism, local schoolchildren were given a five-day holiday for the event; loudspeakers were erected throughout the city so that everyone could hear the services; Count John McCormack was enlisted to entertain the Papal Legate and other visiting dignitaries. The Eucharistic Congress was, in short, a vast religious jamboree – the ultimate physical manifestation of Catholic Irish identity – and de Valera was at the heart of the proceedings.

When Fianna Fáil came to power, the global economy was reeling from the Great Depression and its attendant hardship. The party remained in office for the next sixteen years. A new industrial policy under Seán Lemass attracted many people from the countryside in search of a more prosperous life. They all needed homes. Fianna Fáil met that need, and the party deserves credit for its early radicalism, although it was the previous government of Cumann na nGaedheal (Fine Gael) that had introduced the key piece of legislation to enable local authorities to start building new homes.

Crumlin and Marino were among the first of many public housing schemes that eventually broke the inner-city slums – but also the inner-city sense of community. Struggling to survive, many Dubliners voted with their feet. De Valera once boasted that to understand the Irish people he only had to look into his own heart. A trip to Dublin airport would have been just as instructive. When the airport opened in 1937, one of its key promoters – Lord Mayor Alfie Byrne – boasted that 'airmindedness' was a thing of the future. He was not wrong. Many Dubliners bought one-way tickets.

Dublin had once enjoyed an international reputation for the quality of its equestrian statuary. After independence, such monuments became easy targets for twitchy nationalists. In 1929, the statue of William III on College Green was blown up by republicans, and in 1937, the IRA blew up a statue of George II in the centre of St Stephen's Green. The space once occupied by the statue is still empty, except for a modest flowerbed. Potential replacements have included the Virgin Mary and Jack Charlton, with the obligatory mention of Patrick Pearse, Maureen Potter and Boyzone. At the time of writing, the plot remains vacant.[4]

Women in the Free State

The new Irish constitution was published in 1937, after many months of correspondence between Éamon de Valera and the president of Blackrock College, John Charles McQuaid. The *Dictionary of Irish Biography* has the details:

> [McQuaid] supplied de Valera with documentation relating to papal encyclicals, philosophy, and theology. Some of this material influenced the articles of the constitution relating to personal rights, the family, education, private property, religion, and the directive principles of social policy. However, his proposed

---

4   To visit the centre of the Green is a disappointing experience, like opening a lazy present. It is a bit dull, like any monument to the sensitivity of Irish history, but the centre of Dublin's greatest park is also a potential source of national pride. This sacred site awaits a champion.

religious clause, which declared that the catholic church was the 'one true church' was rejected by de Valera and the team of officials who were drafting the constitution, much to McQuaid's disappointment.

The constitution was progressive in some ways, and McQuaid was partly sidelined, both by de Valera and by the great John Hearne, the main drafter, who created a pretty robust Bill of Rights at a time when Europe was descending into fascism. Still, this body-building statement of national principles was not *un*influenced by the Catholic Church.[5]

An early advertisement for the Electricity Supply Board has the woman of the house relaxing because 'the laundered things [are] crisp and snowy, and the food easily and perfectly cooked'. Dev would have approved. In his God-fearing Ireland, a wife needed her husband's signature to get a passport, and she had to retire from her civil service job as a teacher or a nurse, say, after getting married. From 1935 to 1979, it was illegal to sell contraception.

Even those women who had fought for Irish freedom were routinely denied the prizes afforded to their male counterparts. Margaret Skinnider was shot three times during the Easter Rising. When she applied for a military pension in 1924, she was refused on the basis that she was a woman. The government told her that pensions were for 'soldiers as generally understood in the masculine sense'.

---

5   Shortly after the document was published, an anonymous woman wondered aloud (in the letters page of a newspaper) when someone would admit that it is physically harder to wash a tub of clothes than to draft a constitution.

The Trade War

In the 1930s, Éamon de Valera is remembered for doing some good things, like introducing the legislation that would give Margaret Skinnider a pension, and rehousing the poor of Dublin. He also fought an economic trade war with the United Kingdom. His obsession with self-sufficiency led to a bizarre policy that penalised the Irish people for having a neighbour. And Britain was the state's largest trading partner. Protectionism wasn't just dubious history. It was dreadful economics. Dev's romanticist agro-primitivism was a disaster. One result was mass emigration – typically to the United States or England.

De Valera wanted to rid Ireland of English influence. He failed. Consider the suburban town of Dún Laoghaire, where the terraced houses and seaside views could be mistaken for the seafront in Brighton or Blackpool. Carew Street is so English that the Spice Girls decided to film a video there. These aren't quirks of geography. They speak to the unique heritage of Dublin as the second city of the British Empire.

The critic Brian Fallon wrote, 'Ireland's social revolution produced its full quota of ambitious pace seekers and scheming mediocrities, who rapidly formed a new Establishment and even a new conformity.' That conformity was policed by the state and a Church that was all but ubiquitous. It could be a very dull place.

Could one escape? Yes and no. When the writer Maeve Brennan moved from Dublin to New York, she saw two nuns on a street near Sixth Avenue and was suddenly returned to her time in a convent boarding school, where 'the sight of a nun would fill me with apprehensiveness and dislike'.[6] In New York it was 'miraculous to be able to be so free … no wild survey of a panicky conscience'. Yet half of Brennan's short stories are set in and around her childhood home in Cherryfield Avenue, Ranelagh. In these memorable fictions, Brennan dissects middle-class Dublin without pity or affection.

In the mind of Éamon de Valera, Dublin was synonymous with the old enemy, but it was also problematic because de Valera could never be described as the most popular politician in the capital. That honour belonged to a Home Rule dinosaur.

King Alfie

In 1930, after seven years without a representative municipal government, Dublin Corporation was restored and enlarged to include Pembroke, Rathmines and Rathgar. Alfie Byrne was the first lord mayor of Greater Dublin. For nearly a decade he would rule the city, turning a symbolic position into a civic good. 'I know half of Dublin,' he quipped, 'and the other half knows me.'

Byrne had far less power than his top hat suggested, for the balance of power had shifted since 1922 from City Hall to the Custom House, where the Department of Local Government was spreading its wings. Public housing investment by the local authority would expand, but it was always going to be under the eye of the departments of Finance and Local Government. The state checked the ambitions of the Corpo.

---

6   In 1934, Maeve Brennan's father, Robert, was appointed as the Irish representative in Washington DC.

In 1930, Alfie Byrne was appointed as the first lord mayor of Greater Dublin. A huckster for civic pride, he encouraged the city to see itself as larger and more inclusive, but also as smaller and more intimate. Everyone in Dublin knew Alfie.

Byrne kept the title of mayor for the next nine years, at a time when the slums were largely cleared and 10,000 new homes were built for the poor of Dublin. Byrne would have readers believe that he put the roof on every one of those homes. Playing the press better than any politician of his generation, his nicknames included Alfred the Great, King Alfred and, eventually, the Lord Mayor of Ireland. The comedian Jimmy O'Dea called him the Shaking Hand of Dublin. Visitors to the Mansion House were given a box of Alfie-branded chocolates, and even when he said the wrong thing, it only added to his reputation. On one occasion, Alfie Byrne promised to put shoes on the footless.

Byrne's appearance seemed old-fashioned and faintly comical long before his death. A relic of Home Rule, he was famously approachable ('Call me Alfie') and appeared to have no secrets. Today, if you mention his name to older Dubliners, a smile may cross their lips. 'You mean Alfie?' But Byrne was far more complicated than this folksy image suggests. A workaholic loner, who sent 2,000 Christmas cards, the so-called 'Children's Lord Mayor' was an absent father to his own eight children. A conservative devoted to the care of the poor, he hosted Blueshirt rallies in the Mansion House but refused to host a communist event in the same venue. A patron of the Hospital Sweepstakes, even hosting the draws in the Mansion House, Byrne was also a ticket agent, with a man employed in an office across the road. Into this mixture the reader is invited to put unusual verbosity and a pathological horror of jazz, which Byrne regarded as a menace to civilisation.

To be fair, Alfie Byrne was also a champion of the poor. He consistently spoke out about problems in housing, jobs, public health and the treatment of young offenders at a time when Official Ireland seemed indifferent or even hostile to such concerns.

In 1937, eleven-year-old children were being sentenced to spend up to five years in an industrial school for the so-called crime of stealing a few apples from an orchard. When Byrne spoke out about such 'savage' sentences, a judge responded with a bullish defence of the industrial school system, urging an end to 'ridiculous Mansion House mummery'. But Byrne stood firm. 'For the punishment of trifling offences,' he said, 'the home of the children is better than any institution.' If these words seem mild, consider the context. The mayor was taking on the judiciary, the government and the Catholic Church, which operated many of the industrial schools, at a time when critics in Ireland were quickly silenced.

Byrne was about to get his comeuppance.

That autumn, the lord mayor of Dublin set his sights on becoming the first Irish president. The *Evening Mail* called him a shoo-in, but they were wrong. The Catholic primate of all Ireland, Cardinal MacRory, made a decisive intervention, arguing that the new president should be someone above the cut and thrust of normal politics. Fine Gael and Fianna Fáil came together for a day-long conference to nominate an agreed candidate. Shafted by some of the most powerful forces in society, Byrne saw the new position go to his old friend Douglas Hyde. It is natural that de Valera would rather gift the Irish presidency to a Roscommon-born Protestant than a Dublin Catholic; particularly one who had dared to attack the Church in public; particularly one called Alfie Byrne.

Douglas Hyde was a good fit for the role of president, but the meaning of the contest was not lost on Byrne. He went into the political wilderness for the next fifteen years.

Dublin Goes to Hollywood

Over 40 million Americans have Irish ancestry. In the annals of emigration, Dublin figures largely as a point of departure, but most Irish-Americans are descended from the people who were forced to leave from other parts of Ireland during (and after) the Famine years of the nineteenth century. Among those who endured the miseries of a Famine Ship were William Ford, the father of carmaker Henry Ford, and the twenty-six-year-old Patrick Kennedy, great-grandfather of John F. Kennedy.

While the story of the Irish in America is often presented as a straightforward rise from adversity and prejudice to prosperity and prominence, emigrants faced an uncertain future. Some did okay. Many floundered. ('No Irish need apply.') A few excelled. They are warmly and widely remembered.

Irish-Americans have decorated popular culture as music superstars, matinee idols, impresarios, playwrights, actors and singers. Here is something tangible that speaks to the richness of the oral tradition. Alfred Hitchcock, Gene Kelly and James Cagney had Irish blood; Rex Ingram and John McCormack spoke with Irish accents; Eugene O'Neill mined a dysfunctional Irish family for theatrical gold; Gabriel Byrne wrote one of the best Dublin memoirs. The tradition is long, unending and fruitful, and it mirrors the essential condition. Leaving for America remains one of the most sincere expressions of Irishness. Making sense of that abjuration is a fruitful career path.

Three Dubliners who prospered in the world of enter-tainment cannot be said to represent the totality of the Irish experience in the United States, nor even the totality of the Irish experience in showbiz. As women who were public successes, they were all quite unusual. Perhaps Mary Manning, Geraldine Fitzgerald and Maureen O'Hara represent nothing but themselves and the benefit of a good start in life. They grew up in middle-class southside Dublin – within a mile of each other – in the early years of the twentieth century. They each went to the United States and found a larger audience; they each came home in old age; and they each died in their nineties after lives full of colour, drama and public service.

Mary Manning

Mary Manning was born in 1905. Educated in Alexandra College, she studied acting under the legendary actress Sara Allgood at the Abbey Theatre, and founded *Motley*, a short-lived but influential arts journal. Micheál Mac Liammóir once observed that Manning's 'brain, nimble and observant as it was, could not yet keep pace with a tongue so caustic that even her native city was a little in awe of her'. Manning found fame as a playwright on the stage of the Gate Theatre in the 1930s before emigrating to America, where she married a Harvard law professor, had three daughters and introduced America to the work of Samuel Beckett and Brendan Behan.

When Manning's husband died, she returned to Dublin, becoming a waspish, widely read drama critic for *The Irish*

Times and a popular presence around the city. Mary Manning hosted a birthday party in her retirement home shortly before her death at the age of ninety-three.

Geraldine Fitzgerald

Geraldine Mary Wilma Fitzgerald was born in 1913 on Leeson Street. Educated at convent schools and the Dublin Metropolitan School of Art, this diminutive figure – she was five foot three inches tall – began her acting career in the Gate Theatre before moving to London, where she enjoyed success in films.

In 1938, Fitzgerald returned from the screen to the stage. On Broadway she excelled in George Bernard Shaw's *Heartbreak House* (Fitzgerald is thought to have had an affair with her co-star Orson Welles, another ex-Gate protégé) and was quickly signed up for a contract by Warner Brothers. Her first American film was a classic. Starring opposite Laurence Olivier in *Wuthering Heights*, Fitzgerald was rewarded with an Oscar nomination for Best Supporting Actress.

Marrying an heir to the Macy's department store, Fitzgerald moved to Manhattan, though she continued to make films and, in time, theatre. She campaigned to rid the theatre of its elitist tag, and her work with a community theatre company was formally recognised by the city of New York.

In 1981, Geraldine Fitzgerald returned to the Olympia Theatre in Dublin to direct the European premiere of a play, *Mass Appeal*, with Niall Tóibín and Barry Lynch. That same year she played the tipsy billionaire grandmother of Dudley Moore in *Arthur*.

Forthright and idealistic, Fitzgerald straddled the worlds of public service and entertainment with consummate ease. She died in New York at the age of ninety-one.

Maureen O'Hara

Maureen O'Hara was born in Ranelagh in 1920. Her father was a part-owner of Shamrock Rovers football team, her mother a clothes designer and actress. All six of their children were tutored as performers. Maureen went to school with the Sisters of Charity in Milltown and joined the Abbey Theatre. At the age of nineteen, she won a beauty contest in the Gaiety Theatre, whereupon the actor Charles Laughton offered her an acting contract, cast her in *Jamaica Inn* (which would be directed by Alfred Hitchcock) and changed her name from Fitzsimons to O'Hara because it needed less room on a cinema marquee.

In 1941, Maureen O'Hara joined many Abbey alumni in the ensemble cast of John Ford's Welsh coal-mining epic *How Green Was My Valley*. Set in Wales, the film is quintessentially Irish in a way that suggests the mutability of Irishness. It beat *Citizen Kane* to the Best Picture Oscar in 1942.

The coming of colour was a blessing for Maureen O'Hara: with a head full of red hair, hazel eyes and high cheekbones, the Queen of Technicolour went on to make over sixty films. She had a tempestuous relationship with John Ford, the legendary Maine-born director whose parents had emigrated to the United States from Spiddal; he made cinematic art from his own conception of Irishness. They made five films together, including *The Quiet Man*, in which O'Hara's fighting with the actor John Wayne is a proxy for another man's passion: 'That was real dung in *The Quiet Man*. He was the biggest devil, John Ford. He put as much of that dung in the field as he could, and then made sure that I was covered in it by the end of the day. Oh, I can still smell that awful stuff.'

In 1968, O'Hara married a famous pilot, Charles Blair. They lived in the US Virgin Islands, where Blair set up an inter-island airline service; after his death, O'Hara became the first female president of a US airline company.

O'Hara was the first American citizen to have the nationality Irish – as opposed to English – recognised in her citizenship paperwork. In 2011, she gave a signed photograph to the Little Museum of Dublin, inscribing it 'to all my fellow Dubliners'. Maureen O'Hara died at the age of ninety-five in 2015. She was recently voted as the greatest Irish film star of all time.

The Emergency

Between the two World Wars, many European countries succumbed to extremist governments of the far left or the far right. However, the Irish were suspicious of life on the political margins. This is not to say that temptations did not arise from time to time. In the 1930s, de Valera was forced to ban the quasi-fascist Blueshirts, a private army that was intimately associated with his political rivals in Fine Gael.

The Blueshirts – or the Army Comrades Association – were led by Eoin O'Duffy, a bombastic figure who presented himself as an easy answer to communism. Impressed by the rhetoric of fascism, O'Duffy dressed like Benito Mussolini and looked like Homer Simpson. The founder of the Blueshirts was a bigot and a hypocrite. Anxious to embody the tightass moralism of Catholic Ireland, this outspoken critic of smoking, drinking and effeminacy in young Irishmen was himself a chain-smoking, alcoholic homosexual. He found bogeymen lurking in every shadow and was prone to hysterical flights of fancy. To the credit of the fledgling Free State, this pantomime villain was soon ushered off the stage.[7]

Officially, at least, Ireland stayed neutral during the Second World War – or the Emergency, as it was known – although the state and most Irish people were more sympathetic to the Allied powers than Nazi Germany. Dubliners were issued with gas masks and rationing was introduced, another challenge to hard-pressed mothers. Sugar, tea, butter, margarine, bread, flour and clothing were among the many items for which ration tickets were required. Poor families were hardest hit by the restrictions as bread was a central part of their diet. However, the most unpopular figure in the city was not the Minister for Supplies, Seán 'half-ounce' Lemass, but the notorious 'glimmer man' who went door-to-door to ensure that Dubliners were not using gas after hours.

Throughout the war, Dubliners nailed metal tips into the soles of their shoes, to save the leather. The sound of a large crowd walking down O'Connell Street was said to be a minor sensation. In the Little Museum, there is a leather bingo card that was used by the Butchers Social Union for their weekly bingo

---

7   By the way, threats to the security of the state also came from the extreme left. As taoiseach, de Valera sanctioned the execution of several former comrades in the IRA. And in the Second World War, the IRA would disgrace itself by cosying up to the Nazis.

games – but the cards kept going missing. The bingo players were taking the cards home to patch holes in the soles of their shoes. So the organisers decided to stamp holes in the cards.[8]

The classic view is that the Irish huddled in a dark cave during the war and at the end of it they came out of the cave, blinking into the sunshine. Faintly touched by the conflict unfolding around it, the capital appeared remote and provincial. But the war was not without cost to Dublin – a German bombing on the North Strand claimed the lives of twenty-eight people – and the city was probably less provincial than it appeared on the surface.

Wartime Dublin has been described as the Casablanca of the north. Nonsense. (This is what happens in Dublin when a tall tale is stretched beyond breaking point. The facts just snap into place.) But the city *was* home to some colourful exiles, such as poet John Betjeman and physicist Erwin Schrödinger, along with spies, refugees and displaced persons. De Valera was instrumental in bringing Schrödinger to Dublin. The Austrian physicist ended up living on Kincora Road in Clontarf with his wife, daughter and mistress. Their poor cat was left back in Austria, both alive and dead.

What does it mean to be Irish? One answer is to obey strict limits of identity. On St Patrick's Day 1943, de Valera gave a broadcast on Raidió Éireann in which he shared a vision of

---

8   Shoes feature in another example of local opportunism. The Winstanley factory near Christ Church made expensive dress shoes for the American market. Most Dubliners couldn't afford them, but if there was even a tiny scratch on the leather, the shoes had to be sold for a pittance. Many children had the privilege of wearing Winstanley seconds.

The physicist Erwin Schrödinger spent seventeen years in Dublin. He ended up living in Clontarf with his wife, daughter and mistress. Schrödinger's poor cat was left back in Austria, both alive and dead.

Ireland in the future that is rooted in the past. His reverie was designed for a conservative, Catholic, rural audience. Dublin is not mentioned once. The speech is worth quoting because it is designed to soothe its audience. Outside the capital, this is what people *wanted* to hear in 1943:

> The ideal Ireland that we would have, the Ireland that we dreamed of, would be the home of a people who valued material wealth only as a basis for right living, of a people who, satisfied with frugal comfort, devoted their leisure to the things of the spirit – a land whose countryside would be bright with cosy homesteads, whose fields and villages would be joyous with the sounds of industry, with the romping of sturdy children, the contest of athletic youths and the laughter of happy maidens, whose firesides would be forums for the wisdom of serene old age.

Two years later, in a devout display of Irish neutrality, the death of Adolf Hitler prompted Éamon de Valera to offer his condolences to the German representative in Dublin. His strict adherence to diplomatic protocol caused an international scandal and remains a source of historical debate, yet de Valera's government was largely pro-British. So were most Dubliners.

Jews in the city knew that de Valera was no anti-Semite. He had Jewish friends and repeatedly expressed his admiration for Jews, which makes the government's refusal to allow Jewish refugees into the country after the war all the more frustrating.

There were already 5,000 Jews living in Dublin, and their contribution to the cultural, social and political life of Ireland was out of all proportion to the size of the community. For example, father and son Joe and Ben Briscoe would both serve as lord mayors. Both represented de Valera's Fianna Fáil party.

In 1948 a coalition led by Fine Gael came to power. A new taoiseach, John A. Costello, took the political world by surprise when, during a visit to Canada, he declared that Ireland would leave the Commonwealth and become a republic. In the official account, Ireland would finally stand on its own two feet.

John Charles McQuaid

In 1940, John Charles McQuaid was appointed as the Catholic archbishop of Dublin. Over the next thirty years, he would oversee the construction of eighty churches and over 250 schools in Dublin. When this dynamic conservative spoke in the name of Jesus Christ, no one interrupted. 'His Grace' did not want girls playing hockey because he thought it would make them infertile. He railed against the 'unnatural pleasures' of female gymnastics, and he refused to let boys and girls compete in the same athletics meetings.

Artists, writers and homosexuals often felt unwelcome in McQuaid's Dublin, so they emigrated, or else went into internal exile. In an old formula, artists were stuck 'between the devil and the Holy See'. Imagine fighting a revolution for the country of your dreams and ending up in Catholic Ireland. The writer Seán Ó Faoláin described it as a 'dreary Eden'.

In the 1960s, the brilliant author John McGahern was sacked from his job as a teacher in St John's, Clontarf (Belgrove National School). In the mind of John Charles McQuaid, who ordered his departure, McGahern was an incorrigible pornographer. His seminal novel, *The Dark*, had been banned by the censorship board, and worse, McGahern had married a Finnish divorcée. He had to go.

John Charles McQuaid's relationship with Éamon de Valera eventually broke down over the archbishop's determination to build a cathedral in Merrion Square.[9] Mindful of the significance of the location – right beside parliament – de Valera stood up to McQuaid on that occasion, but the bishop would continue to play a big part in public life. Successive governments had little incentive to upset the social settlement that had been reached with the Church in the nineteenth century.

Today, John Charles McQuaid's extraordinary role in the provision of social and educational services is largely forgotten. He is remembered as yet another cleric whose legacy has been tainted by allegations of inappropriate relations with children.

Getting Out of Dublin

In the early 1950s, over half of Dublin's children left school at the age of thirteen. There was mass unemployment throughout the decade, and women did much of the heavy lifting. Men speak louder in official histories, but in working-class memory, folk heroines outnumber folk heroes. Time and again, mammies tried to hold large Catholic families together, often working several jobs. But one of the children was usually coming or going.

---

9   The park in Merrion Square was known as Archbishop Ryan Park until the cleric was criticised in the 2009 Murphy Report into the mishandling of allegations of sexual abuse in the Archdiocese of Dublin.

More than half a million people left Ireland between 1945 and 1960. Those who stayed behind were not rich. Most of the time, they were broke. This is not to imply uniformity. There was a profound gulf between the experience of men and women; between the privileged and the poor.[10]

In 1954, a priest, Father John A. O'Brien, wrote *The Vanishing Irish*, which asked if the Irish were going to vanish from the face of the earth. More recently, a political scientist, Tom Garvin, published a classic study called *Preventing the Future: Why was Ireland so poor for so long?* These book titles are themselves a miniature history of the period.

Most Dubliners fared marginally better than their rural cousins. The 1950s is the decade in which they witnessed the creation of new bus routes, churches and cinemas. Historian Tim Carey has described this trinity – convenient transport, God and Clark Gable – as 'the three essential components of suburban living'. The reader who remembers the opening of, say, the Casino cinema in Finglas can attest to the seismic effect of such a development.

And there was always the Royal.

Everyone loved the Theatre Royal on Hawkins Street. It was the single largest auditorium in these islands. The cine-variety

---

10 The Dublin mammy deserves greater celebration. Take Maureen O'Carroll, who was the mother of Brendan O'Carroll, the foul-mouthed TV star Agnes Browne. Maureen, who had ten other children, led a campaign to bring down the price of staple groceries. She told an interviewer, 'I'll never let a Bachelor Pea in my house again.' In 1954, Maureen O'Carroll ran for the Dáil, becoming the first female Labour TD. In the hustings, she campaigned for female gardaí, putting women on state boards and removing the word 'illegitimate' on a birth certificate.

In the 1950s, Dubliners witnessed the creation of new bus routes, churches and cinemas – 'the three essential components of suburban living'.

format enabled 3,850 Dubliners to see a show and a movie (with a singalong, too) on one ticket. Louis Elliman, the dynamic Jewish impresario, kept the prices low so that everyone could go, and the Royal made stars of Jimmy O'Dea, Maureen Potter and Noel Purcell.

To this day, the Theatre Royal occupies an oversize place in the imagination of the Hibernian metropolis. Older Dubliners have warm memories of the Compton organ that came up out of the ground, conductor Jimmy Campbell and, of course, the famous Royalettes, along with star choreographers Alice Delgarno and Babs de Monte.

All the big stars of the day played the Royal. Judy Garland wowed punters who couldn't get tickets by singing from her dressing-room window. Gracie Fields and Max Miller littered stardust over Hawkins Street, and Danny Kaye was fondly remembered by the taxi drivers of Dublin for many years. He sang so many encores that everyone missed the last bus home.

The Royal was sold in 1962. The closing night is remembered as one of the greatest social occasions in the history of Dublin.

Institutional Ireland

A ledger records the names of the clients in Dublin's largest Magdalene laundry, at High Park in Drumcondra. They include the de Valera family and the president of Ireland. Until quite recently, religious institutions ran orphanages, industrial schools, homes for single mothers and the now-notorious Magdalene laundries.

The laundries were founded as places of respite and training for women, prostitutes in particular. After independence they became places of arbitrary detention: for orphans who had grown up in state care; for cruelly named 'fallen women' who had given birth outside marriage (often as a result of rape); for girls who were simply outspoken or even high-spirited.

In the laundries, unwanted women laboured for their keep in illegal and unsafe work environments. They were run with the full support of the state and the Catholic Church, which mediated arrangements, and with the explicit support of the public. These 'refuges' were nothing of the sort; rather, they were emblems of craven conformity on a national scale.[11] And for what? Institutionalising exclusion was a form of structural violence that made inequality worse within Irish society. One cannot even pretend that all this happened a long time ago. The last Magdalene laundry in Dublin closed in 1996.

The cruelty of confining inconvenient people is a blow that continues to reverberate. In making a conscious decision to institutionalise exclusion, the explicit support of the state, the Church and the public is inescapable. When, for example, a Dubliner called Patsy Murphy was growing up in Rathmines in

---

11 In *The Irish Difference*, Fergal Tobin wrote about the social settlement that emerged after the Famine, in which priests and bishops threw their weight around, and politicians largely said nothing: 'That social settlement, with the church at its centre, persisted because it possessed legitimacy. The population consented, connived and submitted to its strictures. It knew about the horrors that were the price paid for it ... People knew, but they looked the other way. Why? Because they deemed it a price worth paying for a society that was stable, peaceful and at ease with itself. The smug petit bourgeois paradise rested on these evils. Yet it rested comfortably.'

the 1940s, she was told to be good or else she would be sent to Goldenbridge, the home of St Vincent's industrial school. Shame was a powerful social stimulant. Be good or be sent away.

Paula Meehan is sometimes called a citizen poet; her work speaks on behalf of people on the margins of Irish society. As she says, 'I commemorate the poor going round and round the bend.' One of Meehan's poems is about a boy who was locked up in Letterfrack industrial school, a boy who found dignity in his own imagination:

> He slept beyond reach of the fists, the lies;
> he dreamt beyond reach of our pity.

The Mother and Child Scheme crisis revealed much about the moral climate in mid-century Ireland. It also illustrated the limits of secular authority in the shiny new Republic of Ireland. When Dr Noel Browne TD proposed free medical care for pregnant women, and children up to the age of sixteen, stern opposition from doctors and the Church led to the scheme's cancellation and Browne's resignation as minister.

Once again, the winning hand was played by John Charles McQuaid, who came out against the proposal. The archbishop spent thirty years as the supreme religious authority in Dublin, and his energy cannot be faulted, for he did his best to prevent the future.[12]

---

12 In 2022, the seven-bedroom home that McQuaid occupied in Killiney was put up for sale with a guide price of €12 million. The archbishop once added a belfry to the property, so that he might see the stars more clearly … or keep a closer eye on Dublin.

So Long, Alfie

In 1954, a stalemate on Dublin City Council enabled Alfie Byrne to become lord mayor of Dublin for a record tenth time. Two years later, when Byrne died at the age of seventy-four, his funeral was the largest seen in the city for many years. Traffic in O'Connell Street was held up for twenty minutes to allow the cortege of over 150 cars to pass; all along the route to Glasnevin cemetery, women knelt in circles, saying the Rosary. Éamon de Valera was not among the mourners.

Alfie Byrne is an awkward presence in the nationalist pantheon. In most histories of Dublin he is simply not mentioned. Most people who drive down Alfie Byrne Road do not know that Byrne was the most popular man in Dublin; a nationalist who opposed the Easter Rising; a proud West Brit who spent forty years arguing for a united Ireland; the last survivor from Westminster; a one-off who created a unique role for himself on the national stage.

No one spent longer than Byrne in the Mansion House; no one else served as an MP, a TD, a senator, a councillor *and* lord mayor of Dublin. He had many flaws, but he also had a powerful effect on civic pride in Dublin. Transcending class and geography, he made the city smaller and more intimate, but also larger and more inclusive.

Crucially, this strange little man turned a role that is largely ceremonial into something more remarkable. This explains why he is still remembered with affection by some older Dubliners.

The Whitaker Reforms

East Germany and Ireland were the only two countries in Europe that saw their populations fall in the 1950s. In one year alone, 1957, almost 2 per cent of Irish people simply left the country.

While the East Germans put up the Berlin Wall, a quiet-spoken mandarin in the Department of Finance, T.K. Whitaker, was creating an export-led strategy for growth. With the support of political modernists like Gerard Sweetman and Seán Lemass, Whitaker recognised that it was time to tear down the walls of the Irish economy. Fintan O'Toole has called him 'the greatest of the conservative revolutionaries', describing him as a man who recognised 'the great paradox of his time: that Ireland could not be stabilised without radical change'.

In addition to being a great public servant, T.K. Whitaker was a modest man. When the Little Museum opened in 2011, Whitaker declined to be represented in the collection. 'I can't think of anything suitable [to display],' he wrote, 'but I hope the museum is a success, and am pleased to enclose a small contribution.' The cheque for €200 that accompanied his letter is now framed on a wall of the museum.

How to Get Around

1. **Planes**: In the 1960s the value of Irish exports tripled on the back of the Whitaker reforms, but unemployment remained high. For a woman in want of a career, air hostessing was often the best option. There is a poster

that looks like an ad for Aer Lingus. It is actually a promotion for Prescotts, the company that dry-cleaned Aer Lingus uniforms. The copywriter borrowed the attendant glamour of air travel to market a laundry in Drumcondra.

2. **Trains**: Dublin is home to the oldest commuter railway line in the world. It facilitated the mass exodus of the middle classes from the city centre. The city also had an extensive tram network, before buses came to dominate the streetscape. The last tram, a No. 8 to Dalkey, left from Nelson's Pillar on 10 July 1949. The Hill of Howth Tramway continued to provide a service until it closed down on 31 May 1959. There were many souvenir hunters. Parts of that tram still decorate the dining rooms of Dublin.

3. **Automobiles**: Public transport made a star of Thomas Dudley, who was known as Bang Bang because he pretended to shoot motorists and pedestrians from the back of buses. 'Bang bang, you're dead!' Dublin played along. A sweet, good-natured person, Tom Dudley may have faced difficulties in his life, but he brought a smile to many faces and earned a place in urban folklore alongside other legendary street characters such as Forty Coats and the Diceman.[13] Such figures deserve to be remembered in this history of a city they entertained.

---

13 The street characters of Dublin are the subject of an excellent book by Rory Campbell, *Walking-Class Heroes*.

Dublin in the 1960s

It is often said that the 1960s did not arrive in Ireland until the 1970s. In reality, consumer culture flourished in the 1960s, free second-level education was introduced, the standard of living finally started to rise, and the arrival of RTÉ television altered the expectations of the young. On *The Late Late Show*, a woman from Terenure, Eileen Fox, said that she wore nothing in bed on the first night of her honeymoon. The clerical establishment was incandescent. 'The Bishop and the Nightie' was one of many coups for Gay Byrne, the original young fogey, who was instrumental in revealing Ireland to itself. This talented broadcaster would eventually become the world's longest-running chat show host.

On 26 June 1963, President John F. Kennedy arrived in Dublin as the first Catholic president of the United States. Thousands of people lined the streets to catch a glimpse of the 'homecoming hero', as *The Irish Times* called him. A local woman once assured the author that it was the first time she had ever seen a handsome man in the flesh; without regular access to good dental care, everyone was, it seems, dazzled by Kennedy's teeth. He represented the glamour of the new world, though his roots were, of course, Irish. Kennedy's great-grandfather had emigrated during the Famine years in the nineteenth century.

Two days later, Kennedy gave an uplifting speech in the Dáil. He chose the occasion to salute George Bernard Shaw in the city of his birth: 'The problems of the world cannot possibly be solved by sceptics or cynics whose horizons are limited by

Many Irish people tried to catch a glimpse of President John F. Kennedy. A local once assured the author that it was the first time she had ever seen a handsome man in the flesh.

the obvious realities. We need men who can dream of things that never were, and ask why not.'

While President Kennedy was assassinated later that year, it is easy to draw the dots between his inspirational words and some of the brighter events of the 1960s, a time in Dublin when television broadened horizons, consumerism was embedded as a social phenomenon, and there was a new curiosity about the culture.

In the realm of live music, the exuberance of the dance halls reflected a broader engagement with the outside world. Traditional music found virtuosic champions in Ronnie Drew and Luke Kelly, whose first performances with The Dubliners took place in 1962 at O'Donoghue's Pub on Merrion Row. A fortnight before the assassination of Kennedy, the Beatles played two legendary concerts in the Adelphi cinema. Traffic came to a standstill on O'Connell Street, as crowds of young Dubliners succumbed to Beatlemania, just like kids all over Britain.

In 1966, traffic came to a standstill on O'Connell Street once again, when an IRA splinter group blew up Nelson's Pillar. It is a pity that some of these nationalists did not live to see the much-loved Pillar's replacement. In the words of an unknown Dublin wag: 'The dead, the dead, the dead! They have left us our Fenian fools!'[14]

The state celebration to mark the fiftieth anniversary of the Easter Rising was equally jingoistic and unthinking. Here was

14 Patrick Pearse entered the public imagination when he addressed the funeral of Jeremiah O'Donovan Rossa in 1915. 'The fools, the fools, the fools! They have left us our Fenian dead ...'

Irish nationalism at its most tone deaf. All that back-slapping had an impact in the North, too, where civil rights protests would soon turn into a thirty-year war between nationalists and the British government.

Finally, a housing crisis prompted a decision to build high-rise social housing in Ballymun. This demands our attention, if not for aesthetic reasons. Seven fifteen-storey towers – each named after a leader of the Easter Rising – and nineteen eight-storey slab blocks were erected in Ballymun, aping the model for British post-war urban reconstruction. The brochure for the scheme featured an artist's impression of children wearing blazers coming home from school. Yet, the towers of Ballymun would become a byword for economic and social deprivation: Ireland's greatest housing scheme was also the state's worst planning disaster. In 1987, U2 wrote 'Running to Stand Still', a powerful anti-manifesto about the fifteen-storey towers with only one way out. The last of those towers was demolished in 2015.

The Destruction of Dublin

The Irish are not visually illiterate. Indeed, the state has produced some fine artists. However, the vernacular architecture is borderline notorious and for a long time many Irish people were ambivalent about saving Old Dublin.

In the 1960s, Georgian Dublin was regarded as a relic of English rule: a foreign place on native soil, like the Eiffel Tower in Las Vegas. The architecture critic of the *Financial Times* wrote, 'The only reason why Dublin remained for so long the beautiful eighteenth-century city the English built is that the Irish were too poor to pull it down. This, unfortunately, is no longer the case.'

On St Stephen's Green, thirty large houses were razed to the ground. The demolition of Kildare Place spurred Desmond and Mariga Guinness to re-establish the Irish Georgian Society. When a group of campaigners occupied a house in Hume Street to stop its demolition, government minister Kevin Boland railed against the 'belted earls and their ladies and left-wing intellectuals' behind this 'open act of piracy'. The protesters were ejected, and in time, the houses were knocked down to build a mock Georgian office development. Great swathes of the city have since succumbed to this convenient 'solution'.

In 1980, *Hibernia* magazine published a cover story about 'The Martyrdom of St Stephen's Green'. After fifteen years of pillage, 'the Green is being dismembered not site by site, but side by side. Its west side is a builders' yard, its east side pastiche and its south side a motorway.' Commentators wrote about the 'rape' of the Green, but Frank McDonald remembers it differently. 'What happened was more like a gang-bang in which the shameless participants kept coming back for more.'

When Dublin Corporation decided to build its new headquarters in the historic core of the city, beside Christ Church, excavations at the site were carried out under Dr Pat Wallace. Thanks to the work of Wallace and his team, we know more about Dublin around the year 1000 than we do of almost any other European town of the time. The four-acre site yielded a treasure trove of ancient wonders. Archaeologist

Linzi Simpson says, 'The remains were astonishing ... the archaeological footprint of many generations who lived in the bustling international port known as Dyflinn.'

The Wood Quay site was integral to the early medieval history of the city. It had to be preserved. A campaign was launched by the Friends of Medieval Dublin, a group of swashbuckling academics led by UCD's Professor F.X. Martin, that resulted in a c. 20,000-strong protest march to 'Save Wood Quay'.[15] The poet Thomas Kinsella told the marchers that Wood Quay was 'the birthplace of our own city'.

On 1 June 1979, fifty-two citizens broke into the Wood Quay site and staged a sit-in for several weeks. It became known as Operation Sitric, after the Hiberno-Norse King of Dublin, Sitric Silkenbeard. But official ears were deaf to the concerns aired by historians, archaeologists, politicians and the general public regarding the preservation of the site. The protestors were forced off the site, and after the Friends of Medieval Dublin lost their legal battles against the corporation, the Civic Offices were built on the site. When the time comes to replace these unlovely concrete blocks, the decision is unlikely to cause much concern.[16]

---

15 The Friends of Medieval Dublin are still active. They research the history, archaeology and heritage of medieval Dublin, with a free-to-attend annual symposium and publications on the latest discoveries.

16 In 2015, Dr Wallace lamented that 'very little now remains of the rich layers which earned Dublin such international fame. In less than half a century, we managed to destroy in one way or another the best-preserved urban archaeological remains of any town in Western Europe.'

Modern Dublin

The old familiar is made new and unfamiliar in Europe. This geographic thought experiment broadens the achievements and the identity of the Irish people. Indeed, that act of becoming European has complicated the experience of being Irish, which now includes exposure to Beethoven, claret and the Eurovision Song Contest. But getting into Europe was not easy.

The bid to join the EEC was a fraught process that required a large measure of courage on the part of many stakeholders. Twice blocked by the French, the outcome was unclear until 83 per cent of the Irish electorate finally voted to join the EEC in a referendum in May 1972. It was the greatest expression of pooled sovereignty since the foundation of the state.

The results of the experiment have surprised even the most panglossian Europhile. Goods exports topped €1 billion for the first time in 1973; that figure now exceeds €160 billion every year, largely due to the success of the Irish service economy and easy access to a market of 500 million consumers.

Dublin has ballooned in size since the early 1970s, with new satellite suburbs in Crumlin, Ballyfermot and Finglas, then a generation later in Tallaght and Clondalkin. All those suburbs mean near-universal commuting and all the attendant anxiety. For most people, living in Dublin means suburban Dublin, an area that now includes places like Balbriggan, Maynooth, Ballyfermot, Blanchardstown and Dalkey.

The city got bigger in the 1970s, but the coming of the purpose-built office building did not result in skyscrapers on the Liffey. Successive governments favoured industrial estates on the fringes of the city, and residential zoning policies also favoured the strengthening of satellite hubs.

In the 1970s, as the North erupted in violence,[1] Charles Haughey emerged as the most visionary and divisive force in southern politics. Dubliners waited six months for a phone line to be fitted, RTÉ television started broadcasting at 5 p.m., and Aer Lingus bought its first four jumbo jets.

Tony Ryan worked for Aer Lingus before launching GPA, an ill-fated airline leasing company, and, later, an airline called Ryanair. This European version of Southwest Airlines is so famous that there is a Ryanair shot in golf. The ball takes off in the right direction but lands nowhere near your destination. But Ryan had the last laugh. The airline he founded in Dublin is now the largest in Europe.

Soccer has deep working-class roots in a city that has produced some world-class footballers (John Giles, Liam Brady and Paul McGrath, to name but three) and it is still home to storied clubs like Shelbourne, Bohemians and Shamrock Rovers. The 1970s was the decade in which Dublin's

---

1   In the Republic, the UVF killed thirty-three civilians in Dublin and Monaghan on 17 May 1974.

Gaelic footballers – coached by the legendary Kevin Heffernan – moved from the margins to the centre of cultural life.

'The Dubs' contested nine All-Ireland finals and won four of them between 1974 and 1985, in the process recruiting a new generation of urban youth to the ranks of 'Heffo's Army'. The rise of the Dubs came to symbolise both a city and a sporting culture in the midst of change. As the capital expanded, so too did the GAA, putting down roots in newly sprawling suburbs.

Liberal Ireland began to find its voice in the 1970s, just as John Charles McQuaid found himself unheard. For most of his life, contraception was a sin; then it became a crime; eventually, it was established as a human right. That is a social history of modern Ireland in one sentence.

A longer history would include a chapter on 1970s' second-wave feminism and pioneering organisations such as the Irish Women's Liberation Movement (forty-nine of its members took the so-called 'Contraceptive Train' to Belfast in 1971), the Council for the Status of Women, Dublin Rape Crisis Centre and the Irish Housewives Association. On Monday evenings, feminists like Mary Maher, Nell McCafferty, Rosita Sweetman and Mary Kenny met for dinner in Gaj's, a Baggot Street restaurant.[2] On the agenda: radical transformation in societal attitudes to the family, sexuality, religion and education.

---

2   Rosita Sweetman says that women had little or no control over their own fertility in the early 1970s. 'The Pill was not allowed, except as a "cycle regulator" for middle-class, married ladies if you were lucky enough to have a sympathetic doctor and lived in Dublin. An Irish solution to an Irish problem.'

Dublin owes some of its liberality to the taboo-shattering achievements of these women.

Two icons of Old Ireland, McQuaid and de Valera, died in the 1970s, but the Church still had muscle: divorce and abortion remained illegal, homosexuality was a criminal offence until 1993, and it was only after a referendum in 1995 that divorce was legalised. When Pope John Paul II came to Dublin in 1979, it is said that 1,250,000 people attended a Mass in the Phoenix Park. That was over a third of Ireland's population. The baby boom of the 1970s peaked nine months after the Pope's arrival. The result includes many lads called John, Paul and John Paul. The economist David McWilliams christened this generation the Pope's Children.

By the 1980s, Catholicism was like Bernie Madoff at a fintech conference: rich and powerful, but morally bankrupt. A litany of revelations about clerical child abuse has since undermined the authority of the Church in Ireland and many other countries.

Bob Geldof, Bono and the Live Aid Generation

The 1980s in Ireland are synonymous with elections, unemployment and yet more bombs in the North. But it was also the decade of the Live Aid concerts, in which Bob Geldof of the Boomtown Rats introduced his personality to 1.9 billion viewers.[3] It is not true that Geldof said, 'Give us your fucking money' on live television, although the sentiment is all his

---

3   Bob Geldof's mother, Evelyn, worked as a cashier in the Theatre Royal.

Bono is not universally admired, but at his best – on stage in Dublin, New York or Las Vegas – the U2 frontman enables his bashful compatriots to perform their Irishness.

own. U2 delivered one of the most memorable performances in Wembley Stadium, and Live Aid raised over £150 million for famine relief in Ethiopia.

The career of U2 singer Paul Hewson is a speciality subject of any Dubliner who was born after 10 May 1960. This can be challenging. Bono is like an annoying older brother who makes the news every time he goes to work. A gifted performer with (by his own admission) a Messiah complex. An artist with the soul of a great salesman. The most famous Irishman alive today, he lives in a mansion in Killiney.

The U2 frontman is not just a rock star at home in Mc-Gonagles and Madison Square Garden. He is an older sibling to a town full of grumblers, grovellers and couldn't-care-lessers. When one figure is an enduring presence in the lives of so many others, he is bound to make mistakes, and it is not always easy to walk in his shadow, but Bono's talent is irrefutable.

'Sunday Bloody Sunday', 'Where the Streets Have no Name', 'Bad' – these are not songs. They are chapters in our social history. U2 makes many people proud to be Irish and some people proud to be Dubliners. At his very best – standing on a stage in Dublin, Sydney or Las Vegas – Bono enables his bashful compatriots to *perform* their Irishness.

Dublin on its Knees

Nelson Mandela called the Irish one of the leading Western nations in the anti-apartheid movement. He was referencing the Henry Street Dunnes Stores strike against handling South African fruit. The strike started in 1984, when shop attendant

Mary Manning told a customer that she would not handle any fruit or vegetables from the apartheid state. Mary and eight colleagues went on strike for the next two and a half years, surviving on strike pay of £21 a week. Archbishop Desmond Tutu supported the strike, and as a result, some priests refused to shop in Dunnes, while sympathetic customers left full trolleys at the checkout stands, a tactic that was later borrowed by protestors in South Africa. Eventually the Irish government banned the sale of South African fruit and vegetables.

In 1985, Frank McDonald's *The Destruction of Dublin* was published. This scathing account of municipal corruption and incompetence galvanised readers. A few months later, the Dublin Crisis Conference called on the government to 'accept that the city is in crisis'. The Fine Gael–Labour coalition introduced the Urban Renewal Act, with tax incentives to encourage development in neglected areas.

By 1987, the economy was on its knees once again. Wags said the trendiest place in town was the queue for visas in the American Embassy. That year, Roddy Doyle self-published a novel called *The Commitments* about the unlikely rise of a soul band from the northside of Dublin. Doyle needed a bank loan to print the book, and to get the bank loan he had to write a business plan, which was a greater piece of fiction than the novel.

In 1988, Dublin Corporation decided that the city was a thousand years old. The millennium ('D'aluminium', as Dubs put it) was a well-meaning con, because no one knows exactly when the place was founded. However, with the help of a catchy slogan – Dublin, be Proud – and milk-bottle branding, the city really *was* great in '88. Civic pride is the amount of goodwill that a place has for itself. Often overlooked, it has an economic impact, and can even serve as a bulwark against the excesses of nationalism. In 1988, Dublin took the time to give itself a hug. The value of such a civic benediction may be hard to measure but the positive memories are real enough.

The Giddy Decade

The Irish have a long tradition of celebrating failure. They cherish calamity in the same way that other nations celebrate their success. As William Butler Yeats once said of a friend, 'Being Irish, he had an abiding sense of tragedy, which sustained him through temporary periods of joy.' In 1990 the Irish soccer team offered one of those temporary periods of joy, when they 'won' the World Cup, by losing to the hosts, Italy, in the quarter finals.

Italia '90 enabled Dublin to make an exhibition of itself. It hardly mattered that the Irish team did not actually win the World Cup, in a poor-quality tournament that yielded fewer goals per game than any World Cup in history. Work and social routines were cast aside; there was carefree singing and dancing with strangers in the street; unconscious outpourings of pride in an Irishness untainted by problematic politics or religion. As the journalist Con Houlihan put it some time later, 'Sorry, I missed Italia '90, I was in Italy at the time.'

The prophet who took the Irish to the promised land was an Englishman. It is not literally true that Big Jack Charlton gave the team and everyone else the self-belief to kickstart the

Celtic Tiger, but the delusion is widely cherished, which gives it folk legitimacy.

A few months later, Mary Robinson from Ranelagh became Ireland's first female president.[4] At 6 p.m., RTÉ television would broadcast the Angelus, a minute of prayer before the news, but that evening, the Angelus was abandoned in favour of the new president's victory speech. Robinson tells the story of a woman whose husband asked her for a cup of tea the next morning. But the woman said no. 'Things have changed around here,' she said. 'Make it yourself!'

The hands that rocked the cradle *had* rocked the system. And things *were* changing. In 1991 the Virgin Megastore was prosecuted for selling condoms. By 1994, condoms were freely available and homosexuality was decriminalised. In 1996 the last Magdalene laundry closed down.[5]

In the 1990s, after many years of economic illiteracy, the Irish economy finally started to grow, and it continued to grow by 7 per cent for seven consecutive years. Dublin felt like a gold-rush town in which the man who drives the biggest car is universally hailed as a genius. In this vacuous climate, an event of real substance occurred. Some politicians put away their grievances.

The Good Friday Agreement of 1998 marked the end of the Troubles, the thirty-year period of terrorist- and state-sponsored

---

4   Robinson was born in Ballina but ended up living on the southside of Dublin.

5   One hundred years ago, 3 per cent of Irish university students were women. Today there are more women in college than men, and half of the lecturers are female. Irishwomen have fought for contraception, divorce, equal pay, maternity leave and marriage equality.

violence in the north of Ireland.[6] Nearly 4,000 people were killed in the Troubles. Unspeakable horrors were committed in the name of the Irish people. The Good Friday Agreement brought clarity to the subject of belonging by inviting all of the people on the island of Ireland to embrace a multitude of identities. Suddenly it was okay to be multi-hyphenated. Old certainties were replaced by new hope.

The optimism of the boom[7] found full expression in *Riverdance*, an Irish dancing extravaganza that heavily leaned into the idea of the Global Irish. Emigration and renewal are among the central themes. Dublin born and bred, this stylish exploration of Irishness has delighted audiences all over the world. The director of the show, John McColgan, is invited to a lot of weddings, as love blossoms within a large, friendly cast. At the time of writing, there are sixty-nine *Riverdance* couples and 120 *Riverdance* babies. Three *Riverdance* babies currently work in *Riverdance*.

Helicopters to Punchestown

Horse racing has always been one of the most popular things to do in Ireland. In 2008, there were 1,200 helicopter landings

---

6   The Good Friday Agreement is sometimes called the Belfast Agreement.

7   In the first years of the new millennium, the Scottish writer Andrew O'Hagan taught in Trinity College. Dublin was a 'far-fetched' city that reminded him of Calcutta: 'full of nice British buildings, with too many people for its size, too many cars, and a rather steep inner-city distinction between the newly rich and the old-fashioned poor ... The glory is the Georgian squares, the talk of books, the neon signs, the poetic force of the drama, the jokes, the soda bread, and a general fair-play attitude that makes everybody seem accountable and nobody secluded from what is best and worst in the Irish day.'

In 2008, there were 1,200 helicopter landings at the Punchestown horse-racing festival. The following year, there were 300 landings. Renards nightclub was a casualty of the crash.

at the Punchestown horse-racing festival. The following year, there were 300 landings. The overheated construction industry came to a standstill, public-private partnerships to regenerate run-down corporation flat complexes collapsed, a generation emigrated, the economy went into a nosedive, and the government ended up asking the European Union, the European Central Bank and the International Monetary Fund to organise a bailout. To complete the immiseration of Dublin, the once-fashionable Renards nightclub closed down in 2009.

The Irish are sensitive to the charge that everyone lost the run of themselves. In 2012, then-Taoiseach Enda Kenny was lambasted for saying the crisis was the result of Irish people going 'mad with borrowing'. In his book *Moneyball*, the American author Michael Lewis wrote, 'Left alone in a dark room with a pile of money, the Irish decided what they really wanted was to buy Ireland. *From each other.*' Ireland's financial disaster was created, he observed, 'by the sort of men who ignore their wives' suggestions that maybe they should stop and ask for directions ...'

If history has taught the Irish anything, it is to pretend that everything is okay when visitors are in the house. So the capital was sparkling when Queen Elizabeth II arrived for a state visit in 2011. Not since the fourth visit of Queen Victoria in 1900 had the city paid such a lavish tribute to the old enemy. The smell of paint was overpowering.

In Dublin, Queen Elizabeth bowed her head for the men and women who died to secure Irish independence. The Queen had to say that Britain and Ireland were more than friends but avoid overstepping the bounds of friendship by saying something incendiary. She started in Irish: 'A Uachtaráin agus a chairde.' ('President and friends.') What history will remember is that London and Dublin articulated and then enacted a sincere reconciliation. The first time in a century that a British monarch had been welcomed to Ireland, it felt like a demonstration of maturity, because of what was said and the language in which it was said, but also because of the strategic omissions: the old scabs left unpicked. The demands of the moment were deemed to be more important than the grudges of the past. And then came Brexit.

Dublin in a Tweet

The greatest historian of Dublin, Sir John T. Gilbert, was the son of an English Protestant and an Irish Catholic. In his long, rolling prose style, Gilbert reminds us that history is complex and multivarious. There are always good reasons for complicating the narrative. Pieties are unhelpful when it comes to understanding what the present felt like *in* the past. And scholars have an obligation to make history legible. Gilbert favoured big words and sonata-length sentences in a history of Dublin that extends to three volumes. The demands of the present are more concise. It is brevity that defines this challenge. Can the story of Dublin be told in a tweet?[8]

It is certainly possible to capture the *shape* of history in just a few sentences. Long before the digital age, Christine

---

8   Can you tell the story of Dublin in a few words? Please tweet your response
     to the Little Museum of Dublin.

Longford summarised Dublin in forty-three words: 'Dublin is a city of contradictions and survivals,' she wrote. 'Its biography is not the history of Ireland. Its character has been developed by successive invasions, by prosperity in the eighteenth century and decay in the nineteenth, and by political independence at the present day.'

But this is a lot of words. Let's raise the stakes by bringing the number right down.

For the architectural historian Christine Casey, the story of the built fabric can be summarised in just three themes: river, rivalry and revolt. In an interview before his death in 2023, the publisher Fergal Tobin also chose three themes:

1. **Religion:** 'The failure of the reformation was very unusual in the European context, in that the king could not make his writ run here … Irish Catholicism got away with it.'
2. **Distance:** 'Dublin is farther away from the centre of British power than we think. London has always been looking across the Channel. As the crow flies, Charing Cross is closer to Amsterdam or Brussels.'
3. **Class:** 'Once the Gaelic lords were defeated at the Battle of Kinsale, and the old English, the Hiberno-Norman descendants, who remained Catholic at the Reformation, once they were defeated at the Boyne and Aughrim, Ireland had no domestic ruling class. The fabled Ascendancy didn't do their job after the Act of Union. There was a huge vacuum of social leadership.'

For the scholar Kevin Whelan, the magic number is not three but four. In Whelan's conception of the urban fairytale, there are four little pigs. As he explained in a Gilbert Lecture for Dublin City Council:

> We all know the story of the three little pigs. I've got four little pigs this evening. And it's about the city of Dublin as being a city of wood, then a city of brick, a city of words, and finally, I want to talk about it as a silicon city. So my four little Dublin pigs are wood, brick, words and silicon.

Whelan argues that silicon enabled the transformation of the Grand Canal Docks: as a result, Dublin is now home to the European headquarters of Facebook, LinkedIn and Google. David Dickson contextualises the same information by pointing to the role played by a few individuals in history. He reminds us that it was the persistence of one government executive, Dermot Tuohy, that resulted in Google's choice of Dublin for the company's European headquarters in 2002. 'From Diarmuid MacMurrough inviting the Normans to Dermot Tuohy chasing Google, individuals can sometimes change the course of history.'

If the function of this parlour game is to capture the sweep of Dublin in a few points – let us agree to disagree on three – one might begin by saying that the Irish capital is an only child; continue by admitting that its people are related to everyone; and finish with the irrefutable tweet that books are the family business.

1. **Dublin is an only child.**

   It has no full siblings. Even today, after a century of independence, it is not really an English city, but it's not not like the country it represents, either. No one looks up to Dublin.

2. **The people are related to everyone.**

   In a melting pot that is also a place of refuge, many people have roots elsewhere, be it Scandinavia, Britain, America, Poland, France, Ukraine or Africa. Dubs are mongrels. Even the 'locals' have one foot in the country.

3. **Books are the family business.**

   It is weird that a small city should produce three Nobel Laureates in Literature. Dublin is properly famed for its conversation and, in turn, its writing.[9] That heritage encourages authors to dissect the longings of the heart in every age.

The Fragile Future

In 1922, just 3 per cent of people who lived in Ireland were born outside the state. Today the figure is 17 per cent.

As the engine house in one of the most globalised countries on earth, the city's openness to outside influences is one of the things that gives the silicon age its charm (see: Capel Street on a Friday night). *Dubh Linn* is not a village on the banks of the Liffey anymore. The second most widely spoken language in the city is not Irish. It is Polish.

---

9   This book includes an appendix on the writers of Dublin.

There is much to celebrate about post-pandemic life in the capital of a secular republic with a free press, fair elections and an independent judiciary; a place where freedom of speech is taken for granted by the locals and prized by immigrants from less liberal societies. Why are those celebrations so muted and irregular?

Because Dublin is an only child. There is a minister for rural Ireland, but there has never been a minister for Dublin. The capital is responsible for half the jobs in Ireland and 40 per cent of the tax revenue, but the municipal government has little clout. On the national airwaves, the city is rarely admired, for fear of upsetting the natives. Here is Dublin as a stranger in a strange land.[10] History as current affairs.

Dublin also has a dysfunctional relationship with itself. Many residents think of the city as two towns separated by a river. This northside/southside divide is a shibboleth, encouraged by the delightful satire of Ross O'Carroll-Kelly. 'On the northside they cut the grass. On the southside we mow the lawn.' The real economic divide, between east and west, is ignored by people so small they can't get over a river.

Such behaviour speaks to what Sigmund Freud called the narcissism of small differences. Narcissism is unhelpful because the challenges of the moment are acute. They include war in Europe, a housing crisis at home and climate change everywhere. An uninhabitable planet raises serious questions

---

10   The bourgeois Dubliner is rather like the proud Irish speaker. These faux-aristocrats are conditioned to hate each other, but they have a similar reading of Irish society. The nation throws its eyes to the ceiling when you enter the room. If you were any less acceptable, you would have two heads.

about the future of the city's water, energy and food supplies, and about the openness that makes Dublin so attractive to people from all over the world.

In this high-speed history of the riverside village that became the capital of a dynamic European democracy, it is tempting to conclude that nothing can stop Dublin from bouncing back, because it has done so in the past. But progress is not inevitable. At the time of writing, late-stage capitalism has yet to prove itself capable of extinguishing a large house fire. While the Hibernian metropolis is more remarkable than its critics believe, the city may also be more fragile than its champions imagine.

Appendix

The Writers of Dublin

Dublin is an only child. Dubliners are related to everyone. And books are the family business. As such, authors matter. Their opinions count in a way that often surprises visitors. You can keep all your learned economists; honestly, no one listens to them; it is writers who are asked to calculate the longings of the human heart. The privileged position that they enjoy is a proof of the native gift for communication. The Irish are a nation of champion storytellers. In Dublin, that tradition finds its apotheosis. We celebrate those who say it best. And in return, they populate the city with fictional characters. A good puzzle would be to cross Dublin without meeting a literary ghost.

The local dialect, Hiberno-English, is said to be a souped-up vehicle for delineating the peculiarities of human experience. There is some truth in this grandiose claim.[1] To have a native

---

1   Pub bores often claim that Hiberno-English is the purest form of English spoken in the world. This proves that a lot of tosh is spoken in the pubs of Dublin. In truth, the English of Donnybrook or Donabate is no more or less pure than the English spoken anywhere else. And yet ...

Dublin is a powerful place where literature goes to reimagine its own possibilities from time to time.

tongue replaced by a foreign language; to take that language and make it slightly better; to create revolutionary new ways of documenting life; to turn a tiny city into a global capital of literature; collectively, this a formidable achievement. What makes it remarkable is that the Irish state has often opposed the production of art, working – in deference to the Catholic Church – to discourage and even punish writers for having the temerity to speak their minds.

This miniature study of writing by and *about* Dubliners does not pretend to be comprehensive. There is, for example, a rich tradition of writing in Irish. And the focus of this project is not to catalogue the suburbs but the idea of Dublin itself, which means 'between the [Royal and Grand] canals' in the literary imagination. The indulgent reader should be left with a sense of the ink-stained city as a character in its own story, as well as the role of books in the local culture, and a few of the names who matter. The survey begins with a toast to an immortal quartet.

Jonathan Swift, Oscar Wilde, William Butler Yeats and James Joyce put Dublin on the literary map of the world. Swift was the author of *Gulliver's Travels* and a folk-hero of the poor. Wilde was the greatest comedian of the nineteenth century. Yeats wrote some of the most memorable lines of poetry in the English language. And Joyce wrote *Ulysses*. Everyone writes in their shadow. For everyone, read: 'everyone'. In Dublin, you are no one until you have written a book, or, as Dubliners pronounce it, a *buke*. The Irish capital regards the empty page in the same way that a gravedigger approaches the funeral of a celebrity. It is just another hole to be filled.

The Primary Journey

Jonathan Swift made his name as a Tory propagandist in London before returning to his birthplace, where he served as dean of St Patrick's Cathedral and perfected his satire. Today we remember him for works like *Gulliver's Travels* and *A Modest Proposal*. Famous for cataloguing the delusions of his age, that great champion of liberty dares future generations of Dubliners to imagine something more beautiful and more than just an ordinary city. 'Power is no blessing in itself, except when it is used to protect the innocent.'

Swift used language in a revolutionary new way, but there was nothing original about his decision to make his name in London. That journey from the second city of the British Empire to the first is the primary expedition in Anglo-Irish literature. London changes the way that Dublin writes before Dublin changes the way London writes. This is not to suggest any great deference towards the larger city. After Swift – the early master of 'savage indignation' – the Irish voice is often raised in protest against the iniquities of English rule. As time goes by, the cackles become louder.

In the eighteenth century, a contempt for propriety found its voice on the London stage, and the theatre-going public could not get enough of it. Oliver Goldsmith found fame by teasing society, 'the very pink of perfection' as he put it in his famous comedy *She Stoops to Conquer*. Another Dubliner, Richard Brinsley Sheridan, entered the antechamber of the immortals with *The Rivals*, a play that features Mrs Malaprop ('He is the very pineapple of politeness'), a character so good that she gave her name to a new word in the English language.

Maria Edgeworth and Thomas Moore made the journey to and from London in the early years of the Union. (Another great Dublin poet, James Clarence Mangan, was born in the Liberties and hardly ever left, though he was an oddity for many reasons.) Later in the nineteenth century, Irish voices were particularly prominent in English journalism. Fleet Street and Grub Street were synonymous with the Irish in a way that is both startling and hard to comprehend. Paddy took the English language and made it his own.

By the 1890s, George Bernard Shaw and Oscar Wilde were giving the English plenty to laugh about in the West End. At the beginning of that decade, Wilde was the darling of the West End. In *A Woman of No Importance*, Gerald says, 'I suppose society is wonderfully delightful.' Lord Hillingworth replies, 'To be in it is merely a bore, but to be out of it simply a tragedy.'

At his best, Wilde is like an angel tasked with the creation of a new set of rules for the universe. But he is also a keen psychologist: 'Only dull people are brilliant at breakfast.' Or this: 'The world is a stage, but the play is badly cast.' Or this: 'Some cause happiness wherever they go; others, whenever they go.' Is there a more precise slight in the English language?

The Icarus-like Wilde had a tragic fall from grace, and eventually he was sentenced to spend two years in prison for the crime of sodomy. On his release he went to Paris, where he died at the age of forty-six, on the doorstep of the twentieth century. This thoroughly modern Dubliner still speaks to us *and for us* in language that never grows stale.

George Bernard Shaw left Dublin as a teenager. His affection for Ireland did not extend to its capital, yet he never lost his Dublin accent, and his memory of the slums would inform his politics forever. 'The lack of money is the root of all evil.' In London, Shaw became famous for ridiculing the pretensions of the English. The self-styled downstart was unafraid of giving the *bourgeoisie* the lashing they craved. 'We have in England a curious belief in first rate people, meaning all the people we do not know. This consoles us for the undeniable second-rate-ness of the people we do know.'

The Joyce Problem

James Joyce left Dublin at the age of twenty-two, vowing never to return, yet wherever he lived, Joyce wrote only of his birthplace. The clarity that distance provides would inform the greatest novel of the twentieth century. How did this artistic revolutionary nail the Irish condition? By leaving. As he put it himself, the shortest way to Tara was via Holyhead.

In *Dubliners*, Joyce created the finest collection of short stories in the English language. This is not to say that Dublin is flattered by a book in which its own Boy Wonder diagnosed its problems. 'I think people might be willing to pay for the special odour of corruption which, I hope, floats over my stories.' Dublin was the setting, he said, because it was 'the centre of Ireland's moral paralysis'. As an introduction to the genre, the city or the country it represents, *Dubliners* remains essential reading.

In *Ulysses*, Joyce captures every inch of Dublin. His great novel, the 'cracked looking-glass of a servant', complicates life in the city because a genius got there first. To this day, lovers fumble in the shadow of Joyce, who set his masterpiece on the day the author first walked out with Nora Barnacle. *Ulysses* may well be a story about the majesty of ordinary life, but the book makes every first date insignificant. Thanks to Jim Joyce, one cannot walk into eternity along Sandymount Strand. One can hardly have a glass of Burgundy and a Gorgonzola sandwich in Davy Byrne's without walking into his ghost. Precious? So is time. Haunted by the memory of this polymath for the ages, the temptation is not to write but to say nothing.

(Some people wish that Joyce had kept his own mouth shut. When *Finnegans Wake* was published, *The Irish Times* concluded that the novelist had no more to say after *Ulysses*. 'In *Finnegans Wake* he went on saying it.')

To the Pub

In *Ulysses*, Joyce's alter ego, Stephen Dedalus, muses, 'Good puzzle would be cross Dublin without passing a pub.'[2] To develop a literary culture, it helps to have a lot of good pubs. In Dublin, they are the natural habitat of the writer, and the setting for its oldest joke.

---

2   This challenge is almost as demanding as getting to the end of *Ulysses*. After a few drinks, most Dubliners will admit that they have read the first page of Joyce's masterpiece. In the Little Museum, a copy of the first edition is left open on the last page, so that visitors can say they have *finished* reading *Ulysses*.

– What are you doing?
– Writing a novel.
– Neither am I.[3]

Dublin is the home of Guinness, of course, and it remains difficult to cross the city without passing a pub. Even the cultural quarter, Temple Bar, is known by locals as the Temple of Bars. Publicans have made good money off many writers, including Brian O'Nolan, Flann O'Brien and Myles na gCopaleen, who were all the same person, though it was said that he drank enough for all three.

Jonathan Swift once observed that taverns sell madness by the bottle. Oscar Wilde called work the curse of the drinking classes. Brendan Behan described himself as a drinker with a writing problem. He said God created alcohol to stop the Irish from ruling the world. At the time, he was probably holding court in McDaid's. When the pub was sold, a Dubliner quipped that the ship was deserting the sinking rats.[4]

---

3   Irony often features in the humour of Dublin. The street poet Pat Ingoldsby tells a story about a local urchin who refused to buy a book of his poems.
    'Those poems are shite,' said the young man.
    'Have you read them?' said Ingoldsby.
    'No,' he replied. 'I don't need to read those poems to know they're shite.'
    Ingoldsby describes this sentence as the most Dublin thing he has ever heard.
    Another incident that captures the vernacular humour: a man assures a lockhard (an unofficial parking attendant) that he doesn't need anyone to keep an eye on his Range Rover because there is a big dog in the boot. The lockhard asks, 'Does your dog put out fires?'
4   It is not exactly true that all great Dublin writers were habitués of the public house. William Butler Yeats did not like pubs, and George Bernard Shaw

Behan and the Monaghan-born poet Patrick Kavanagh were friends before a bitter falling out. In a literary journal, Kavanagh lamented the provincialism of middle-class Catholic Dublin. He once wrote that provincials have no mind of their own, because they are always trying to ape foreign customs. 'A provincial,' he said, 'is always trying to live by someone else's loves, but a parochial is self-sufficient.'

Like Joyce, Kavanagh went looking for the universal in the particular. Unlike Joyce, he stayed in Dublin, where he drew a distinction between the 'provincial', who looks over his back to see what London is doing, and the 'parochial', who looks for gold in the mud of Monaghan or Dublin or wherever one starts and ends a stanza.[5]

Kavanagh and Behan feature as outsize characters in two definitive literary memoirs: *Remembering How We Stood* by John Ryan and *Dead as Doornails* by Anthony Cronin. Ryan was a scion of the family that owned the Monument Creameries; a publisher, publican and friend to all poets of the day, his memoir is a classic of the genre that might be described as anecdotage. Patrick Kavanagh, Flann O'Brien and Brendan Behan knocked around with both authors in a scene that will be parodied in the same pubs this evening.

Cronin was a barrister, poet and critic who remembered everything. Ryan and Cronin were at the first formal Bloomsday celebration in 1954, when Patrick Kavanagh and the rest of

---

was a teetotaller. When Shaw called whiskey 'liquid sunshine', he did so with a clear head.

5   The critic Declan Kiberd once observed, 'Dublin was a centre dominated by the cultural values of the peasant periphery.'

the entourage got so drunk that walls disappeared. Behan's biographer, Ulick O'Connor, set the scene like this: 'Dublin to an alcoholic is like a girls' gymnasium to a sex maniac.'

Humour and Humanity in a Cold Climate

The puritanism of the new Ireland was informed by nationalism, but it was the Catholicism of its leaders – and their deference to Church leaders – that made the moral climate so inhospitable to the quirky. Many writers voted with their feet ... by leaving town. Joyce and Beckett went to the continent. Sean O'Casey, the brilliant playwright who captured the humours and tragedies of tenement life, spent his final three decades living in England.

And the writers who stayed often went into internal exile. Present, yes, but neither relevant nor welcome outside the pubs, where many writers drank themselves into posterity. Brendan Behan was dead at forty-one. Kavanagh lasted a good deal longer, though his spirit was crushed by the conservatism of Catholic Ireland long before the poet entered old age. In the drama of Dublin, life is presented as a comedy with a poignant ending. Three Protestant playwrights reference the phenomenon in language that deserves to be remembered.

1. Sean O'Casey said, 'That's the Irish people all over – they treat a serious thing as a joke and a joke as a serious thing.'
2. George Bernard Shaw: 'The heart of an Irishman is nothing but his imagination.' In this conception of the

human body, life is a cosmic joke at God's expense. You have to laugh.

3. Samuel Beckett wrote a play called *Waiting for Godot* where nothing happens, twice. He redefines gallows humour as a plea for humanity itself: 'You must go on, I can't go on, I'll go on.' These triplets fall over the sadness of the world. 'Try Again. Fail Again. Fail better.'

Here is the native pose in triplicate. And it is important to remember that the throwaway nature of such observations was indeed a pose. Ultimately, it is not Beckett's deadbeat glamour that we celebrate but the depth of his humanity.

It has often been said that Irish writers work not simply in isolation, but also in opposition to their peers. This mutual disdain is epitomised by what Joyce is alleged to have told Yeats on their first meeting: 'We have met too late; you are too old to be influenced by me.' It was Yeats himself who attributed this line to Joyce, and the older man was no stranger to Dublin's trademark chippiness. He once lamented 'the daily spite of this unmannerly town.'

Closer inspection reveals the depth of fellow feeling between the great Dublin writers. The biographer Richard Ellmann observed that each of them drew from a well of literary kinship. He tells us that Wilde invited Yeats to Christmas dinner in 1888, and that later, Yeats campaigned in defence of Wilde at the time of the prosecution for indecent behaviour. Fast forward a few years, and Yeats is meeting Joyce's train at Euston Station at dawn; after giving the young man breakfast, he brings him to meet several editors.

'Another scene is of Joyce sitting silent but sympathetic beside Beckett's hospital bed after Beckett had been stabbed,' writes Ellmann. 'And there is Beckett's surprise and pleasure when, on first meeting Yeats, the poet quoted approvingly some lines from Beckett's *Whoroscope*.'

Poetry After Yeats

Eavan Boland once described Dublin as 'made for poetry'. The daughter of a diplomat, Boland spent her formative years away from Ireland, but returned in her late teens, which was 'like being dropped into a story with no chapter headings'. Her poetry charts a journey from town ('The Huguenot Graveyard at the Heart of the City') to the southside suburbs, 'the noise of a new Ireland'. Boland and poets such as Pat Ingoldsby, Paula Meehan, Brendan Kennelly and Paul Durcan anatomised the private lives of Dubliners, and in the process, they proved that there is abundant life after Yeats.

Eavan Boland is often mentioned in the same breath as Thomas Kinsella, who said Dublin was where he learned 'to look at the world through the rich reality of the inner city – a living history, with shades of Swift and Emmet in my neighbourhood'. In his poetry, Kinsella could be scathing about the values of modern Ireland:

> Our watchful elders have exchanged
> A trenchcoat playground for a gombeen jungle.

The Outsiders

There is another tradition within the literature of the city. It is the sound of the outsider. Being a prickly race, the Irish do not always like to hear this conversation.

Outsiders describe the capital as a place that is jarringly different from the country it is supposed to represent. Dublin is represented as a figure marooned in alien territory. Here is Christine Longford, who was born in Ireland but left for England as a child, writing in her book, *Dublin*:

> The names of the streets are written in Irish as well as English; but the people seem to speak English, and the Nelson Pillar is a monument to an English hero. In the beautiful library of Trinity College he [the visitor] sees the Book of Kells, a masterpiece of Irish art, but can trace no connection between it and its surroundings. In the Bank of Ireland, which was once the Parliament House, he sees in the House of Lords a tapestry recording the victory of a Dutch king over a Scottish king in Ireland.

In exploring this idea of Dublin as a place that is foreign even to itself, it was a Belfast-born poet, Louis MacNeice, who pointed out that Dublin is not Irish, but it is not exactly English either:

> Fort of the Dane,
> Garrison of the Saxon,
> Augustan capital
> Of a Gaelic nation

In his great poem *Dublin*, MacNeice says something worth repeating about the long span of history. Seeing everything, the city is never shocked. It is ready for your post-traumatic stress disorder, your Pakistani mangoes and your hen parties from Birmingham. Keep them coming.

Olivia Robertson was born in Surrey in 1917. A cousin of the poet Robert Graves, she was first taken to Ireland as an eight-year-old child. 'The new Dublin and I were born at about the same time and, even as a child, I had the pleasant feeling that my country and its capital city were experimenting in living and learning, as I was.'

Robertson wrote a memoir, *Dublin Phoenix*, about growing up in the Free State. 'At [boarding] school in England I had difficulty in persuading my best friend to come to stay; she was afraid of being shot.' The book has none of what Robertson calls 'the unwashed Freudian gloom' of a Joyce short story. 'Dublin has changed. Our new Dublin is not an eyrie for genius: it is a home for ordinary people.' The egalitarian spirit is worth celebrating, although Joyce got his reply in first. The everyman Leopold Bloom could hardly be more ordinary.

Writing in the 1950s, Robertson is loyal to the state but frank about its mistakes ('I deplore the new housing estates that ring round the splendid old city') and cannot understand why the Irish would want to copy all the English faults. 'Alas, the new estates were only too painfully like the Reigate I had left behind me.'[6]

---

6   Robertson catalogues the decline of the old order in a tone that is half-maudlin, half-fascinated. 'Perhaps Herbert Park has a sad, thwarted feeling

Later in life, Robertson acquired some notoriety as high priestess of the Fellowship of Isis, a spiritual organisation dedicated to the Egyptian goddess. Her portrait of the city – 'It is the time of ordinary people who for the first time can buy nylon nightgowns as beautiful as any ...' – is not well remembered, though it has the easy charm of Dublin itself.

Honor Tracy came to Dublin from London after the Second World War. Working at *The Bell*, Tracy had an affair with the writer and serial philanderer Seán Ó Faoláin, and later, in a gossipy memoir, she depicted the Irish as a thin-skinned race, living in fear of the Catholic clergy: 'Their arrogance, their pride, their vindictiveness, their greed did not square with what I took to be the mission of a Christian priesthood.' Tracy concluded that the project of the Church was not Christianity at all. It was 'running a country'.[7]

The capital also features as a subject in many American and English coffee-table books. This is a genre in which aristocrats, such as Desmond Guinness and the Knight of Glin, reflected on the desecration and resurrection of Georgian Dublin. Brendan Behan once defined an Anglo-Irishman as a Protestant on a horse. Guinness and the Knight of Glin were more comfortable in the drawing rooms of New York and Dallas, where their titles and steely charm were employed

---

underlying all its colourful freshness because it is still the open-air refuge of Ballsbridge Protestants.'

7   In 2022, the journalist Derek Scally wrote a book called *The Best Catholics in the World*. While promoting the book, Scally observed that to appreciate the full spectrum of Christianity in Ireland, one should consider the Book of Kells *and* the Ryan Report. The latter documented the shameful treatment of children in institutional care.

in the service of good causes, such as the inestimable Irish Georgian Society.

The two greatest coffee-table books about Dublin were the work of an American, a German-American and an Englishman. The first, Flora Mitchell's *Vanishing Dublin*, is a collector's item. The American artist came to Dublin with her family when her father got a job in the Jameson distillery, and she married a scion of that family. Her book, which was published in 1966, captures the city on the cusp of change. Only 600 copies were printed.

The same open-faced quality is evident in *Dublin: A Portrait* (1967) with photographs by German-American photographer Evelyn Hofer and an essay by V.S. Pritchett. There are portraits of figures like the poet Patrick Kavanagh and the actor and writer Micheál Mac Liammóir. Pritchett's text is lyrical but tough. '[Dublin] is the capital of a country mutilated by an artificial boundary.' Once again, the alien identifies the civic predicament with no hesitation. 'This city that looks more like London than any other in the British Isles is also the most foreign, the capital of a foreign country: Cork and Galway men often hold it to be foreign to Ireland itself.'

Here is the recurring idea of Dublin as an only child. But it is also a literary capital of the world, and Pritchett gives us the details. When the Englishman was visiting William Butler Yeats in his Georgian townhouse, the poet threw a pot of old tea leaves out of the first-floor window. 'Suddenly he went to the Georgian window, opened it and swooshed the tea leaves into Merrion Square.' Here is the history of Dublin in a single careless gesture.

Dublin informs the work of its biographers in the way a flea helps a dog to scratch. Consider the career of J.P. Donleavy, who served in the US Navy before arriving in Dublin to study at Trinity College. Donleavy perused the underworld in the company of his friend Gainor Crist, a drunken charmer who was also studying on the GI bill. Their friendship fills *The Ginger Man*, a classic novel that has the distinction of having been banned in the United States *and* Ireland.[8]

Putting on a show is a Dublin thing to do. Describing a dinner party in 1731, the artist Mary Delany wrote, 'There is a heartiness among them that is more like Cornwall than any I have known, and great sociableness.' Christine Longford said that gossip fuelled the 'city of talkers'. It is true that Dubliners use language in a way that is allusive and weaponised. An old friend once greeted the author with the words, 'I saw John the other day. No friend of yours, by the way.' The journalist Stephen Gwynn once measured this phenomenon: 'We all like to believe that Dublin has a charm of its own, which we encourage strangers to explore; and we do our best to entertain them, according to our frugal resources, at the expense of each other's reputations.'[9]

Dublin is a character in the stories of Maeve Brennan and Mary Lavin, who specialised in a form of literary eavesdropping. Maeve Binchy did something similar in a lower register. The

---

8   Having captured the spirit of Dublin, Donleavy decamped to Westmeath and reinvented himself as an Irish country gentleman.

9   On the mailboat from Holyhead to Dublin, Gwynn overheard an English judge telling a Dubliner that it must be wonderful to live in a town where everyone was so witty. 'Ah, nonsense,' said the Dub, 'if you come to dinner with me, I'll find you a dozen people as stupid as yourself.'

great storytellers of modern Dublin[10] include Dermot Bolger, John Banville, Anne Enright,[11] Roddy Doyle, Colm Tóibín, Kevin Power, Tana French, Paul Murray, Sebastian Barry and Sally Rooney. Some of these authors are from elsewhere; most have lived in Dublin; all operate in a culture of neo-puritanism that is equal parts performative and juvenile. The author hesitates to mention that *Dubliners* is the singer Morrissey's favourite book, or that his parents were from Dublin, for example. One cannot situate Morrissey on any map of Dublin, because he was not only the voice of a generation, he was pro-Brexit. That any artist would wish to share their talent with the public in such a climate is itself remarkable.

Famous Seamus

The three Dublin-born winners of the Nobel Prize – Yeats, Shaw and Beckett – are often mentioned in the same breath as a fourth Laureate. Seamus Heaney won the Nobel Prize for Literature 'for works of lyrical beauty and ethical depth, which exalt everyday miracles and the living past'. 'Famous Seamus' lived in Sandymount for many years and taught at Carysfort teacher training college. But Dublin has a relatively small

---

10 There is also a long tradition of autodidactic writing, from *Dublin Made Me* by Todd Andrews to *Goodbye to the Hill* by Lee Dunne. In *Are You Somebody?* the journalist Nuala O'Faolain unpicked the living scars of trauma in the standout Dublin memoir of the last three decades.

11 In Anne Enright's Booker Prize-winning novel, *The Gathering*, the map of Dublin is used, as Chris Morash says, 'as a kind of topographical language to explore generational memory and class mobility'. A sacred, book-length journey from Broadstone to Booterstown.

claim on Heaney's imagination, unlike his blackberry-picking childhood, the subject of his most celebrated poetry. *Here* was an urbane, worldly version of Seamus Heaney.

Paradoxically, the mere presence of a great poet like Heaney flattered Dublin by encouraging the delusion that putting a few old words on paper could be the making of you; and given the way *you* tell a story, you could be famous, just like Seamus. He was all about the town, modest and approachable. The Nobel Laureate down the road.

When Seamus Heaney died in 2013, a local artist called Maser turned his last text message into a piece of street art: *Noli Timere*. It means 'do not be afraid' in Latin. These words now decorate a gable wall on Richmond Street. They speak to the warmth of the accord between Dublin and its writers. But that relationship has not always been quite so benign. For many authors, there was good reason to worry, and often to get out. Dublin has come a long way in a very short time.

When James Joyce died, the Irish government instructed its representative in Zurich not to attend the writer's funeral and refused to permit the repatriation of his remains. If he were alive today, Joyce would moan about the place of art in the culture, like all good artists, but he would also be surprised by the prominence of literature, which is routinely employed as a tool to promote Ireland Inc. To be fair, this is not just lip service.[12] Many artists and writers pay no income tax, and the

---

12 In 2014, when Christy Brown's archive was sold at auction in London, the author appealed for assistance. Diarmuid Morrissey offered to pay half of the €50,000 cost and the National Library of Ireland agreed to put up the rest. The archive was exhibited in New York and is now back in Dublin.

government is piloting a basic income scheme. A century after the publication of Joyce's masterpiece, the state uses literature to talk to itself and to represent Ireland to the world.

Dublin's reputation for literary excellence was recognised in 2010 when it was officially designated as a UNESCO City of Literature. It may be provincial to observe that London has yet to receive the honour – one can almost hear the ghost of Patrick Kavanagh chiding the author – but this fact also illustrates the scale of the achievement.

Baubles are useful. They encourage the state to support the role of literature within the culture. But perhaps the most sincere tribute that Dublin pays to its writers is not the official attention, nor the statues of Wilde and Kavanagh that punctuate a good Dublin walk, nor even the literary street art, but the simple act of cherishing writers' opinions. They are still taken seriously in Dublin in a way that seems almost heretical in a consumer economy. If, say, a figure like Colm Tóibín is not quoted on the scandal *du jour*, a Dubliner will surmise that he must be away teaching American students how to write novels that subtly alter our perception of reality. Such deference confirms the true status of literature within the Inkpot City, and it speaks to a local speciality, for the writers of Dublin have not only made it a literary capital of the world. They also bring us to a closer understanding of who we really are.

Chronology

This is not an exact chronology. Some of the dates are questionable, but the form is broadly contained within these show-off years.

Foundation

c. 550–650   Monasteries are built in Ireland.

c. 650–700   Irish canon and vernacular law written.

841   A Viking fleet overwinters in Dublin.

975   Brian Boru becomes King of Munster.

980   The King of Meath frees the slaves of Dublin after the Battle of Tara.

997   Brian Boru and Máel Sechnaill (then High King of Ireland) agree to divide Ireland between them.

999   Brian Boru defeats the Leinstermen and the Ostmen at the Battle of Glenn Máma. Sitric Silkenbeard, King of Dublin, submits to Brian Boru.

1014   Brian Boru is killed at the Battle of Clontarf.

1022   Death of Máel Sechnaill.

1028   The first bishop of Dublin is appointed. Dublin has a population of about 4,000.

1102   Dublin's slave trade to Bristol is prohibited.

Anglo-Norman Dublin

1166	Death of Muirchertach Mac Lochlainn, High King of Ireland. Diarmait Mac Murchada, King of Leinster, enlists the help of Henry II.
1169	Wexford taken, Mac Murchada restored to kingship of Leinster.
1170	Marriage of Strongbow to Diarmait's daughter Aoife. Dublin is captured.
1171	After Diarmait's death, Strongbow becomes lord of Leinster. Henry II arrives.
1175	Treaty of Windsor between Henry II and the High King of Ireland, Ruaidrí Ua Conchobair, who agrees to rule unoccupied territory as a vassal.
1185	The future King John visits Ireland.
1204	Construction of Dublin Castle begins.
1210	King John returns, submissions of Irish kings.
1229	Dublin gains a mayor. Population is *c.* 8,000.
1348	The Black Death arrives, killing a quarter of the city's population.
1394–95	King Richard II comes to Ireland. Defeat of Leinster Irish under Art MacMurrough, and submission of nearly all Irish and rebel English chiefs.
1487	Lambert Simnel is crowned as Edward VI in Christchurch Cathedral.
1494	Henry VII sends Sir Edward Poynings to Ireland as lord deputy. Poynings' Law makes English law applicable to Ireland and requires the king's approval for any legislation passed by the Anglo-Irish parliament.

Sixteenth Century

1525	Plague throughout Ireland, particularly in Dublin.
1534–36	Kildare Rebellion: Lord FitzGerald leads a revolt against English rule.
1536–37	Reformation Parliament sits in Dublin.
1541	Henry VIII declared King of Ireland. Ireland is elevated from a lordship to a kingdom.
1548	A charter establishes the city of Dublin as a county borough, clarifying the powers of mayor and sheriffs.
1550s	Plantations established in the midlands.
1551	First book published in Dublin: *Boke of Common Praier*.
1554–55	In Patrick Sarsfield's one-year term as mayor, 'twenty tuns of wine' are consumed; 'his house was so open as commonly from five of the clock in the morning to ten at night.'
1560	Second Reformation Parliament sits in Dublin.
1569–1603	Nine Years' War.
1575	Plague strikes Dublin again.
1580–84	Desmond Rebellion leads to Plantation of Munster.
1589	Sir Francis Drake (allegedly) introduces potatoes to Ireland.
1592	Trinity College Dublin is founded.
1597	Careless handling of gunpowder on Wood Quay leads to an explosion that claims the lives of 126 people.

Seventeenth Century

1604	Plague strikes Dublin again.
1607	Flight of the Earls.
1609	Ulster Plantation.
1637	Dublin's first theatre opens.
1640	The population of Dublin is about 20,000.
1641	Rebellion against British Protestant settlers in Ulster.
1642	Establishment of Catholic Confederation, in Kilkenny.
1649–53	Reconquest of Ireland by English Parliament.
1650	Dublin is struck by plague again and up to half the population dies.
1654–57	Cromwellian confiscations of Catholic-owned land.
1660	Restoration of monarchy; Charles II returns as king.
1662	The Duke of Ormond returns to Dublin as viceroy; the Phoenix Park is laid out as a deer park.
1667	Jonathan Swift is born.
1670	Thatched roofs are banned because of the risk of fire.
1685	Dublin's first newspaper is published.
1690	Battle of the Boyne; Jacobite-Williamite War.
1695	Penal Laws directed at Catholics.

Eighteenth Century

1700	Dublin has a population of about 60,000.
1707	Archbishop Marsh opens library.
1720	British parliament is permitted to legislate for Ireland; St Ann's Church is built.
1726	John Rocque's map of Dublin is published.
1740–41	Famine grips Ireland.
1759	Arthur Guinness opens brewery.
1762	Merrion Square is built.
1773	A body of men is formed to pave, clean and light the streets of Dublin.
1785	In Ranelagh Gardens, Richard Crosbie ascends in Ireland's first manned balloon flight.
1791	The Custom House is finished.
1796	The Grand Canal Dock opens.
1797	James Malton completes his *Picturesque and Descriptive View of the City of Dublin.*
1798	Society of United Irishmen lead an uprising against British rule.
1800	Dublin is the sixth-largest city in Europe, with a population of about 200,000.

Nineteenth Century

1801	Power returns to London with the Act of Union.
1803	Robert Emmet leads an ill-fated rebellion.
1816	The Wellington (Ha'penny) Bridge opens.
1817	The Royal Canal reaches the Shannon.
1825	St Mary's Pro-Cathedral opens. Gas is used to light the streets of Dublin.
1829	Upon securing Catholic Emancipation, Daniel O'Connell is elected MP for County Clare.
1831	The world's fourth zoo opens in the Phoenix Park.
1834	The first commuter railway line opens.
1845	The Catholic University opens.
1845–52	The Great Famine.
1859	*The Irish Times* is launched.
1864	National Gallery of Ireland opens to the public.
1867	Fenian Rising.
1870	First Land Act introduced to reform land ownership in Ireland.
1879–82	Land War.
1881	Arrested for sabotaging the Land Act, Charles Stewart Parnell is imprisoned in Kilmainham gaol.
1882	James Joyce, Éamon de Valera and Alfie Byrne are born.
1890	Dublin Museum of Science and Art (National Museum) opens.
1891	Charles Stewart Parnell dies; *c.* 200,000 people attend his funeral.
1892–1906	A network of sewers is built in Dublin.
1897	Bram Stoker publishes *Dracula*.

Twentieth Century

1904	Bloomsday: James Joyce walks out with Nora Barnacle for the first time.
1913	The Lockout almost brings Dublin to a standstill.
1914–18	Over 200,000 Irishmen fight in the First World War.
1916	The Easter Rising.
1919–21	War of Independence.
1921	Anglo-Irish Treaty is signed in London.
1922	The Irish Free State is formed with its capital in Dublin; James Joyce's *Ulysses* is published.
1922–23	Irish Civil War is won by the new government.
1925	The Monto red-light district is shut down.
1937	New constitution ratified by the Irish electorate.
1939–45	Ireland stays neutral in the Second World War.
1941	Luftwaffe bombs the North Strand, killing twenty-eight people.
1949	A republic is declared in the twenty-six counties.
1959	T.K. Whitaker publishes a programme for economic development.
1961	Television arrives with *Telefís Éireann*.
1969	Outbreak of the Troubles in Northern Ireland.
1973	Ireland joins the European Economic Community.
1976	U2 is formed in Larry Mullen's kitchen in Artane.
1979	Pope John Paul II visits.
1984	DART light rail service begins operation.
1988	Dublin celebrates its millennium.
1998	The Good Friday Agreement.
1999	Gay Byrne hosts his last *Late Late Show* after thirty-seven years.

Acknowledgements

This book was largely written in the home of Susan Jane White. It is dedicated to Susan, with further thanks to our sons, Benjamin and Marty, for indulging my devotion to Dublin.

In the making of the book, the historian Daryl Hendley Rooney spared many blushes; the publisher Conor Graham encouraged me; and my colleagues in the Little Museum, including our CEO, Sarah Clancy, as well as our design team Dara Flynn and Barbara Sangster, played an important role throughout. The work of illustrator Philip Barrett has greatly enhanced the appeal of the text, and I am equally grateful to the excellent team at Merrion Press, including Wendy Logue, Patrick O'Donoghue and Maeve Convery, as well as editor Heidi Houlihan.

Three great friends of Dublin, Frank McDonald, David Dickson and the late Fergal Tobin, encouraged me to write a history at speed. The manuscript was read and improved by friends and colleagues, including Stephen Barcroft, Sarah Clancy, Frank Coughlan, Catriona Crowe, David Dickson, Charlène Duthel, Winter Romanov Hynes, Isabelle Keenan, Conor McComish, Mark McKenna, Neil O'Donohoe,

Diarmuid Ó Gráda, John Ryan, Barbara Sangster, Lina Schmid, Leslie Stepp, Brody Sweeney, Pat Wallace and Tremain White.

Some of this book was written in the Tyrone Guthrie Centre, Newbliss, County Monaghan. This much-loved institution is the most sincere tribute the Irish state pays to the arts.

In the Little Museum, we tell stories about Dublin for the benefit of people from all over the world. A non-profit museum, with a collection created by public donation, our supporters include Dublin City Council, Fáilte Ireland and the Department of Culture. The unpaid board of the museum is led by the chair, Dr Rhona Mahony, and treasurer Brian Geraghty, along with the Lord Mayor of Dublin and Ed Brophy, Miriam Brady, Susan McKeon, Councillor Mary Freehill, Councillor Hazel Chu, James Ryan and Catriona Crowe. The board and management of the museum are determined to build a world-class city museum in the heart of Dublin. If you want to support our work, please make a donation to the museum, which is a registered charity. If you have visited the museum or bought this book, you have already supported our work. Thank you.

Finally, every effort has been made to contact copyright holders. Any mistakes are the responsibility of the author alone.

Further Reading

A writer called James Stephens was born in the Rotunda Hospital on 9 February 1880. Stephens once observed that we are young when the city is old, and old when the city is young. Today, we are asked to share the place with Stephens and many other ghosts, who jostle for space on the streets and dare us to make history equal to the richness of the city.

Stephens was a good friend of James Joyce, who produced a revolutionary new form of biography in *Ulysses*. Of course, Dublin is also the setting for many other triumphs in fiction *and* non-fiction. Here are some of the books consulted in the making of this whistle-stop history. It is a classic Dublin library minus all the glaring omissions. As Joyce observed: 'To learn one must be humble. But life is the great teacher.'

Adams, John, *Dermot MacMorrogh, or The Conquest of Ireland*
Adelman, Juliana, *Civilised by Beasts*
Andrews, C.S., *Dublin Made Me*
Banville, John, *Time Pieces: A Dublin Memoir*
Bolger, Dermot (ed.), *Invisible Dublin*
Bolger, Muriel, *Dublin: City of Literature*
Bono, *Surrender*
Brady, Ciaran, *Histories of Nations*
Byrne, Gabriel, *Walking with Ghosts*
Campbell, Rory, *Walking-Class Heroes*
Carey, Tim, *Dublin Since 1922*
Chambers, Anne, *Portrait of a Patriot*
Cooney, John, *John Charles McQuaid: Ruler of Catholic Ireland*
Craig, Maurice, *Dublin 1660–1880: The Shaping of a City*
Crowe, Catriona, *Dublin 1911*
Cruise O'Brien, Máire and Conor, *Concise History of Ireland*

Cullen, Bill, *It's a Long Way from Penny Apples*

Daly, Mary, *Dublin, the Deposed Capital: A Social and Economic History, 1860–1914*

Delany, Mary, *Autobiography and Correspondence of Mary Granville*

Dickson, David, *Dublin: The Making of a Capital City*

Dorney, John, *The Civil War in Dublin*

Downham, Clare, *Medieval Ireland*

Duffy, Joe, *Children of the Rising*

Ellmann, Richard, *Four Dubliners: Wilde, Yeats, Joyce and Beckett*

Fairhall, James, *James Joyce and the Question of History*

Fallon, Donal, *Three Castles Burning*

Fanagan, Alan, Fanagan, John, and McCarthy, Charlie, *Fanagans of Dublin*

Ferriter, Diarmaid, *The Transformation of Ireland 1900–2000*

Ferguson, Niall, *War, Peace and International Relations: An Introduction to Strategic History*

Flynn, Mannix, *Nothing to Say*

Foster, R.F., *Modern Ireland, 1600–1972*

—, *Vivid Faces: The Revolutionary Generation in Ireland, 1890–1923*

Frazier, Adrian, *Hollywood Irish*

Garvin, Tom, *Preventing the Future: Why was Ireland so poor for so long?*

Geoghegan, Patrick, *Liberator: The Life and Death of Daniel O'Connell*

Gibney, John, *A Short History of Ireland, 1500–2000*

Gwynn, Stephen, *Dublin Old and New*

Hegarty, Neil, *Dublin: A View from the Ground*

Hourican, Bridget, *Straight from the Heart: Irish Love Letters*

Joyce, James, *Ulysses*

Kearns, Kevin C., *Dublin Street Life & Lore*

—, *Dublin Tenement Life: An Oral History*

Kelly, Deirdre, *Four Roads to Dublin*

Laffan, Michael, *Judging W.T. Cosgrave*

Lecky, W.E., *A History of England in the Eighteenth Century, Volume 2*

Lewis, Michael, *Moneyball*

Liddy, Pat, *Dublin: A Celebration*

Longford, Christine, *A Biography of Dublin*

MacMillan, Margaret, *War: How Conflict Shaped Us*

MacThomáis, Éamonn, *Me Jewel and Darlin' Dublin*

McDonald, Frank, *A Little History of the Future of Dublin*

McDowell, Henry, *Irregular Marriages in Dublin Before 1837*

Morash, Chris, *Dublin: A Writer's City*

Novillo-Corvalan, Patricia, *Borges and Joyce: An Infinite Conversation*

O'Brien, Father John A., *The Vanishing Irish*

O'Brien, Jacqueline and Guinness, Desmond, *Dublin: A Grand Tour*

O'Connor, Ulick, *Brendan Behan*

Ó Gráda, Diarmuid, *Georgian Dublin: The Forces That Shaped the City*

Ohlmeyer, Jane, *Making Ireland English: the Irish Aristocracy in the Seventeenth Century*

O'Neill, Ciaran, *The Public History of Slavery in Dublin*

O'Toole, Fintan, *We Don't Know Ourselves*

Pritchett, V.S. and Hofer, Evelyn, *Dublin: A Portrait*

Quinn, James (ed.), *Dictionary of Irish Biography*

Rankin, Deana, *Between Spenser and Swift: English Writing in Seventeenth-Century Ireland*

Robertson, Olivia, *Dublin Phoenix*

Rowley, Ellen (ed.), *More than Concrete Blocks*

Sheehan, Ronan and Walsh, Brendan, *Dublin: The Heart of the City*

Somerville-Large, Peter, *Dublin, the Fair City*

Spinks, Lee, *James Joyce: A Critical Guide*

Stephenson, Tristan, *The Curious Bartender's Whiskey Road Trip*

Tobin, Fergal, *The Irish Difference*

Tóibín, Colm, *Mad, Bad, Dangerous to Know*

Tubridy, Ryan, *JFK in Ireland*

Wallace, Patrick, *Viking Dublin: The Wood Quay Excavations*

Yeates, Padraig, *Lockout: Dublin, 1913*

Index